DOUGLAS JOHN HALL

BOUND
ᴬᴺᴰFREE

A THEOLOGIAN'S JOURNEY

Fortress Press
Minneapolis

Cover design: Lecy Design, Inc.
Book design: Becky Lowe

Library of Congress Cataloging-in-Publication Data
Hall, Douglas John, 1928–
 Bound and free : a theologian's journey / Douglas John Hall.
  p. cm.
 Includes bibliographical references.
 ISBN 0-8006-3773-9 (alk. paper)
 1. Hall, Douglas John, 1928– 2. Theology—History—20th century. 3. Protestant
churches—Doctrines. I. Title.
 BX4827.H244 A3
 230'.044'092—dc22
                         2005010172

Manufactured in the U.S.A.
09   08   07   06   05   1   2   3   4   5   6   7   8   9   10

Bound and Free

"Douglas John Hall's reflections on his journey as a theologian are a treasure of instruction and inspiration. If you want to learn from one who has lived through fascinating times in theology and integrated life and thought in a theology of the cross with wisdom and humility, read this book!"

JAMES M. CHILDS, JR., Edward C. Fendt Professor of Systematic Theology, Trinity Lutheran Seminary

Also by Douglas John Hall

Lighten Our Darkness:
Towards an Indigenous Theology of the Cross

God and Human Suffering:
An Exercise in the Theology of the Cross

God and the Nations,
with Rosemary Radford Ruether

Thinking the Faith:
Christian Theology in a North American Context

Professing the Faith:
Christian Theology in a North American Context

Confessing the Faith:
Christian Theology in a North American Context

Why Christian?
For Those on the Edge of Faith

The End of Christendom and the Future of Christianity

The Cross in Our Context:
Jesus and the Suffering World

Imaging God:
Dominion as Stewardship

The Steward:
A Biblical Symbol Come of Age

Contents

For Rhoda

Her children rise up and call her blessed;
her husband also, and he praises her.
                                    —Proverbs 31:28 rsv

I did not learn my theology all at once,
but I had to search deeper for it,
where my temptations took me.
—*Martin Luther (1483–1546)*

Would-be theologians . . . must be on their guard
lest by beginning too soon to preach
they rather chatter themselves into Christianity
than live themselves into it
and find themselves at home there.
—*Søren Kierkegaard (1813–55)*

Make me a captive, Lord,
And then I shall be free.
—*George William Martin (1828–81)*

Preface

In the introduction to his intriguing story *The Alchemist*, Brazilian author Paolo Coelho writes, "We all need to be aware of our personal calling. What is a personal calling? It is God's blessing, it is the path that God chose for you here on Earth. Whenever we do something that fills us with enthusiasm, we are following our legend."[1] For more than half a century by now, I have felt that it was my "personal calling" to be a Christian theologian. I think I understood that from the first—that is, from the point in the twentieth year of my life when I began at last to comprehend, a little, the Christian message. For better or worse, I knew even then that I could not be only a *hearer* of that message; I would have to try to *understand* it.

It did not take me fifty-plus years to know that I would never understand it fully—or even adequately. At best, I could only *stand under* it, hoping for glimpses and intimations of a Truth that I could neither possess nor skillfully articulate.

Whether or to what extent I have succeeded in grasping even such glimpses and intimations is certainly not for me to say. I will leave that to others—ultimately to the one Other who is able to cause even our mistakes, our heresies, our silences to praise him. That One, I believe, is merciful—even to theologians.

Out of gratitude to that Source of my enthusiasm for theology and to all the others who have helped me and given me courage to pursue my legend, I wish at the end of this long apprenticeship to try to say something publicly about what I have found this vocation to entail.

Among these others (I could never list them all in this place), the following should be acknowledged in connection with this small publication. I am grateful to Bishop Margaret Payne of the New England Synod of the Evangelical Lutheran Church in America for having invited me to address her clergy on the subject of my own theological journey, and to the Melanchthon Institute in Houston and the Church of the Crossroads in Honolulu for having given me the opportunity to work further on the three addresses that constitute the longest chapter of this book. Appreciation is also due to the Institute for Ecumenical and Cultural Research at St. John's School of Theology in Collegeville, Minnesota, where I delivered the address "Bound and Free" at an occasion on April 20, 2002, honoring the founder of the institute, Father Kilian McDonnell, OSB, and to the editorial board of *Theology Today* for publishing that address (vol. 59, no. 3, October 2002). Similar thanks must go to Trinity Lutheran Seminary in Columbus, where I preached the sermon "Words" as a farewell statement after a memorable semester as guest professor; to Montreat Conference Centre and the series Reclaiming the Text, for which I wrote the lecture "Stewards of the Mysteries of God"; and to the Academy of Parish Clergy, whose Book of the Year award inspired me to write the piece included here as chapter 5, "*De Profundis*: On Going 'Right Deep Down into Life.'"

Special thanks are due to my editor and friend Michael West, who has seen me through several literary labors; to my friend of half a century, Friedrich Hufendiek of Berlin, who read the "Journey" addresses and made valuable suggestions; and to Rhoda Palfrey, the companion of my days and decades, who not only has read and commented upon this manuscript with her usual care and perspicacity, but has borne with patience the long absences from our home that were needed to complete it.

Theology as Vocation

Now you are the body of Christ and individually members of it. And God has appointed in the church first apostles, second prophets, third teachers; then deeds of power, then gifts of healing, forms of assistance, forms of leadership, various kinds of tongues. Are all apostles? Are all prophets? Are all teachers? Do all work miracles? Do all possess gifts of healing? Do all speak in tongues? Do all interpret? But strive for the greater gifts. And I will show you a still more excellent way.

If I speak in the tongues of mortals and of angels, but do not have love . . .

—1 Corinthians 12:27—13:1 NRSV

"And God has appointed in the church . . . teachers. . . ."

The theme of this small book, on which all of its chapters are variations, is theology as vocation. It is intended as a personal statement—the statement of one motivated by the belief that his calling as a human being has been to be a student and a teacher of Christian theology. As such, the book no doubt contains many of the limitations—as well as, I hope, some of the benefits—of autobiographical writing. We have no other *immediate* entrée into human experience than our own, and one's own experience in any field of human discourse is necessarily circumscribed. Perhaps, however, probing deeply enough into the passions, temptations, and aspirations of one's own existence can help others explore their experience as well.

As a visit to any good theological library (or to the Internet) will demonstrate, much attention has been paid in the last half century to the theology *of* vocation. But the thought that theology itself is a vocation, and one greatly in need of support and encouragement in our time and place, is rarely considered.

There was a time when the concept of vocation—being called to a lifework—applied exclusively to religious vocations, particularly the monastic life. Martin Luther, who will make his appearance regularly in these pages, began to broaden the idea of vocation to include not only the ordinary priesthood but also the laity.[1] He believed that God calls people to a great variety of offices in the church and in the world. The mother tenderly nurturing her children and managing her household ought to think of her life in vocational terms every bit as much as a priest or bishop or monk. Work becomes something nobler and more meaningful than mere drudgery when it is undertaken in the spirit of a divine mandate.

Like every commendable theological teaching, this one can, of course, be misused—and it often has been: if you make people think they're obeying a call of God, they'll do *anything* willingly, even gladly! All the same, the Protestant liberation of the idea of vocation from its captivity by monasticism and clericalism must be considered a gain—and also an exhortation, for we have still not appropriated it fully or imaginatively.

One may wonder, however, whether we Protestants might have become so enthusiastic about the universal application of the concept of vocation that we have neglected its specific application within the church as such. To be sure, we still speak of being called to "the ministry," usually meaning the ministry of Word and Sacraments, and most of the denominations have devised ways (some of them excessive) of "discerning" the authenticity of such calls. But beyond that and the ritual appointments of various officers in denomination and congregation, we rarely explore the idea of vocation for its implications in connection with the identification and support of *specific ministries within the church*. Paul, however, recognizes a rather large number of these.

In this book I am concerned with only one of the "divine appointments" Paul names. The teacher (the term *theologian* does not appear in the Bible) is neither higher nor lower than the others. There is only one "higher" category here, and it transcends all actual and possible vocations while challenging all to attain it. I mean, of course, the "more excellent way" that Paul turns to immediately in chapter 13, the way called love (*agape*). Though Paul's numbering scheme in naming the various appointments has the unfortunate consequence in some quarters of suggesting rank or gradation of ministries, there can be no question of hierarchic ordering. To be called to an office within the church does not mean to be elevated to another order of being! The only being that matters here is the common identity of *all* those Paul lists as "members of the body of Christ." If he places teachers third, it is surely only because the two preceding categories—apostles and prophets—have a certain chronological and missiological priority, being the initial witnesses to the gospel upon which everything else depends. Practically speaking (whether the apostle intended it or not—who knows?), it may even be appropriate that the teacher should be third, for his or her work is precisely to help the hearers of the apostolic witness, prophetically proclaimed by those gifted with great spiritual insight, to sort out the meaning of what they have heard and to discover, if possible, how to live accordingly. But this ought not to suggest anything like rank or privilege.

All the same, in so vigorously denying any graded ontological interpretation of vocations, Protestants have tended to court a certain danger on the other side of this topic, and it is no theoretical danger. In fact, it is the typical danger into which so much Protestantism has fallen in its anxious avoidance of anything smacking of an "undemocratic" temptation to distinguish too sharply among offices in the church. That danger is functionalism. In their distaste for a Catholicism that elevated the clergy, making clerical existence almost another species of Christian, many Protestant denominations rushed to the opposite side of the arena and propounded a concept of ministry in purely pragmatic terms. Ministry then is seen as a function, a task, a job—no doubt necessary to order and good government in the church, and no doubt a work for which some are better qualified than others, yet possessing no special quality, no aura of sanctity, no mystique, perhaps not even a sense of "call." One can be grateful for the Protestant cleansing of the office of ministry from unwarranted sacerdotalism, but too often, surely, what was washed away was not just the superficial *accidens* but the very *esse* of the office of ministry: namely, its being precisely a vocation.

Vocation, in the biblical and theological understanding of the term, does not equate to function, task, office, or profession. *Voco—vocare* means to be summoned, and even in secular Latin, it is intimated that the summons comes from beyond the self. In its biblical use, the concept is definitely associated with the summons of the speaking God (*Deus loquens*); it has indeed the quality of an "appointment," as Paul assumes in the passage quoted at the beginning of the chapter—not a very democratic idea! Moreover, if we pay strict attention to the actual instances of this calling in the Old and New Testaments, we shall have to put to rest for good and all any idea that the ministry is a career choice. Far from involving the choice of a path, the typical stories of being called in the Bible—not least that of Saul of Tarsus himself—show how consistently the summoned persons *resist* the call, refuse to hear it, or, having heard it, wish they had not. With more than a little hint of such resistance, the apostle to the Gentiles confesses that his calling is a matter of "necessity"—in Greek, *anangke*, a term used in classical Greek to mean compulsion with a tinge of distress. "For necessity is laid upon me; yea, woe is unto me if I preach not the gospel!" (1 Cor 9:16 KJV).

Since I intend this book to be a personal testimony to the subject of theology as vocation, it will perhaps not be out of place if I introduce an autobiographical note and confess, apropos the foregoing observation about biblical narratives of call, that I have always understood my own call to this ministry as containing a definitive element of *gratia irresistibilis*. And that means, of course, that I have also understood something of the depths of my own continuing resistance. When I was ordained in 1956 in the city of Stratford-on-Avon, home of the renowned Canadian Shakespeare festivals and therefore no stranger to a bit of drama, I did something unintentionally surprising to many in the large congregation and the radio audience (the service was being broadcast locally). We seven ordinands were required to make brief statements about our call to the ministry of Word and Sacraments. The other six ordinands all conformed to the general expectation that such testimonies should emphasize the strength of one's sense of call, one's eagerness to serve God and the church, one's desire to "help people," the deep influence of pious parents or pastors, and so forth. I had, of course, prepared my own statement without any knowledge of what the others would say, and I certainly had no desire to shock anyone. But as I pondered the whole concept of vocation to ministry and considered the biblical and other historical background of this concept, I simply felt compelled to testify to the "it's not exactly my idea" side of this entire experience. While I certainly believed I had in some obvious way *responded* to that call, I felt even more strongly that I was not free *not* to respond. So instead of thanking everyone present for all they had done to encourage my entry into this noble and (as it could still be regarded in 1956) prestigious profession, I found myself drawn inexorably to the twentieth chapter of the prophet Jeremiah—which, with a brief personal exposition, I read as my testimony to my call:

> O Lord, you have enticed me,
>   and I was enticed;
> you have overpowered me,
>   and you have prevailed.
> I have become a laughingstock all day long;
>   everyone mocks me.
> For whenever I speak, I must cry out,
>   I must shout, "Violence and destruction!"
> For the word of the Lord has become for me
>   a reproach and derision all day long.
> If I say, "I will not mention him,
>   or speak any more in his name,"

then within me there is something like a burning fire
  shut up in my bones;
I am weary with holding it in,
  and I cannot. (Jer 20:7-9 NRSV)

Half a century later, I am well aware of the naive enthusiasm (not
to say near exhibitionism) implied in such conduct. At age twenty-
eight, having just graduated from a prestigious American seminary
with very good academic credentials and wearing a fine charcoal gray
suit, I could hardly claim that I felt myself spurned as "a laughing-
stock" or a "reproach and derision all day long." (I think I might have
been modest enough to acknowledge that in my commentary.) But I
wanted, in that very respectable liberal church setting, to bear witness
to the fact that there is such a thing, still today, as being picked up
by divine grace and carried "whither one would rather not go" (John
21:18 KJV). At least, I felt, there should be some acknowledgment that
one's positive response to God's call is accompanied by a good deal of
misgiving, if not actual kicking and screaming.

I doubt that my hearers that night knew quite what to make of
my little oration. But my old grandfather, the most genuinely pious
and humble person known to me *ever*, sat in his wheelchair with a
great-grandson on his knees, listening in his farmhouse kitchen to
the radio broadcast of the service, tears running down his cheeks.
He read his Bible so much during the twelve years of his last ill-
ness that it was finally in tatters. (I have it now and treasure it like a
holy relic.) So when he said to me later, "What you did was *the right
thing*," I knew that he was not just demonstrating filial love, strong
as that was in him. He really knew his Bible, so he knew that the
biblical testimony to the divine call simply has that dimension in it. It
is indeed the decisive dimension, for without it, our tendency to see
ourselves as the "masters of our fate and captains of our souls" very
easily assumes credit also for this turning point in our lives, particularly if it turns out that our ministries may be thought to have some
measure of success (another not very biblical concept).

While the call to the ministry of Word and Sacraments is still
emphasized in most Protestant denominations, the sense of there

being a certain specificity within the vocation to ministry appears to have given way to a kind of randomness. The rhetoric of occasional liturgies and installations notwithstanding, one has the distinct impression that decisions concerning the actual working out of the call to ministry are less a matter of vocation than of practicality and of personal or conciliar determination.

LOST SENSE OF VOCATION

Such an observation seems particularly applicable to the vocation of "the teacher." Not only does the theologian today pursue a rather individualistic course toward his or her settlement in this or that (usually academic) posting, but most theologians appear to consider their work less a vocation than a profession. Or, if they sometimes think of what they are doing as a vocation, it is usually in terms barely distinguishable from the casual way in which that term is employed by other academicians or professionals in every field. There are, I think, two somewhat complex and interrelated reasons for this.

Failure to Require Theology and Nurture Theologians

Under the conditions of Christian establishment, there has been (to put it mildly) little demand for theologians within the various church structures as such. But the biblical and Reformation concept of the teaching ministry assumes that it is precisely for the sake of the church that this ministry exists. Its necessity or internal rationale is found not only in the divine will but in the positive need of the disciple community for continuous nurture in the faith. The teacher is not only appointed *by* God but appointed *to* an office within the church. In other words, the biblical concept of vocation has as its *telos* (inner aim) an apostolic rationale. One is not called just to be "a theologian," but to perform a particular service in and for the community of faith—that is, to teach.

In point of historical fact, however, beyond the conventions of seminary training for ministry, the churches have rarely given any conspicuous indication of being keen to have serious theologians in their midst. To the contrary, with few exceptions, they have shown every inclination to avoid theologians wherever possible, including clergy who see their chief role as that of theologians of the congregation. Indeed, one suspects that congregations have been hardest of all on parish ministers who really tried to be (using the Reformed terminology) "teaching elders." Theologians who by their words and actions make it clear that they feel themselves called precisely to serve the churches have often seemed to their denominations to be disturbers of their peace. And here I am not thinking of notorious critics of all things ecclesiastical or of congenitally cranky intellectuals, but of earnest Christian thinkers who tried to keep faith from degenerating into pious froth or thoughtless activism. I would include, among others, most of the renowned theologians of our immediate past, including Karl Barth, Paul Tillich, Reinhold Niebuhr, and Dietrich Bonhoeffer, all of whom were first also pastors and persons whose familiarity with the faith made them expect more of the churches than the churches, on the whole, seemed ready to offer.

Just in this respect, however, the situation seems to be changing significantly. Karl Barth used to refer to "the children's disease of being ashamed of theology." That disease is still all too prevalent in the churches. (I shall refrain from personal testimony to its continuation, but everyone who has tried to exercise a theological vocation in and for the churches will know immediately of what I am speaking.) At the same time, with the increasing disintegration of established Christianity, theology—as I shall say in one of the chapters—is coming more and more into its own as a felt need within the churches. For with the disestablishment of the Christian religion, there comes a new demand for both clergy and laity to search more diligently for "the reason for the hope that is in them." Why, otherwise, would they remain? In short, the need for theology increases as automatic Christianity decreases.

Not only professionally trained theologians are in a position to meet that need. If the church is to survive the winnowing process that has been under way now for two centuries and is accelerating annually, *every* Christian who intends to remain such will be driven to a quest for understanding, the like of which not even the

Reformation produced.[2] All the same, as Paul frankly affirms in the passage from 1 Corinthians, not all are called to be teachers; there is a variety of gifts (1 Cor 12:4-5). The perfecting of these gifts takes time and concentration. In the case of a discipline as philosophically and historically complex as Christian theology, years and years are needed for that refining process.

It may well be, therefore, that as they face more realistically their effective sidelining, the churches will also turn more intentionally toward the teaching ministry. (To a limited extent, this has been happening already.) In that case, the currently rare and random emergence of theologians dedicated to the church will have to be supplemented by a deliberate attempt on the part of ecclesiastical leadership to encourage and support persons in their midst who manifest qualities necessary to the teaching ministry. It may be, too, that more congregations, synods, or other ecclesiastical groupings will seek out theologians who for a longer or shorter period of time could help them find their way into the new and confusing world in which the community of faith today has to live and bear its witness. I have myself, in my retirement, served for a short time as theologian in residence in a congregation that *has* encouraged theology and theologians for many years.[3] I can testify to the enormous difference that is made, both for the congregation and for the theologian serving it in such a capacity, when this kind of ministry is undertaken. The difference is noticeable at every level—liturgy, preaching, social action and community involvement, ethical and moral sensitivity, and the very makeup of the congregation itself. For the theologian, it is a wonderful and liberating experience to discover just how spiritually vibrant, intellectually serious, and politically engaged (in a word, how *real*) Christian theological discourse becomes when it is part of the life of a flesh-and-blood congregation, not just a discipline to be introduced to candidates for ministry and others who are obliged to meet certain academic requirements.

Career-Oriented Intellectualism

If the first reason why the vocation to theology has been insufficiently felt as *vocare* has to do with the church's historic failure to require and nurture theology and theologians, the second must be laid at the doorstep of the theologians themselves. Too many of the best-educated theological, biblical, historical, and other scholars have been "enticed" not by Jeremiah's God but by the kind of intellectualism that thrives in academic settings and by personal ambition. They have seen their vocation not primarily as a call but as a career—and often in quite individualistic terms. Their community of discourse and concern is not a particular denomination or even the ecumenical church broadly conceived, but the academy, with its own well-known system of rewards and punishments, its own language, its own (usually ambiguous) communality. In fact, many who are working in theological or paratheological situations today have little or no connection with institutional religion. They do not write for the churches; they do not write about the churches; they do not seek personal satisfaction or a sense of belonging in that direction at all. I will not say that this accounts for the majority of those teaching theology in North America today, but it certainly accounts for a very large number of them.[4]

Unfortunately, such professionals are prone to condescension in relation to teaching theologians, biblical scholars, ethicists, historians, and others who do consciously attempt to exercise a primary responsibility in and for the churches. The word *popularizer* is often heard in these circles, and there is a kind of unspoken assumption that the scholarship of those who manifest too much concern for the existing faith communities cannot quite be trusted. Such scholarship, it is hinted, is not answerable to the highest standards and betrays too many vested interests to be seriously considered.

No doubt such suspicions are sometimes justified, but membership in the church as such is no more susceptible to bias than membership in academe. As for "vested interests," how could Christian theology *not* have vested interests in the fate of the Christian movement? What kind of theology is it that can be done with little or no concern for its significance among those who—however haphazardly—are trying to understand and live the faith about which the theologians speak and write? Is there not a notorious irony here? For the truth is that most academic theologians in nonecclesiastical settings have the positions that they have because there is still a public demand for religious education that is engendered chiefly by the communities of faith in our society.

The phenomenon of theologians detached from any association with the community of discipleship has become numerically significant fairly recently. In the post–World War II period, in both the United States and Canada, departments of religion suddenly flowered in institutions of higher learning. Therefore, persons graduating from seminaries or university faculties with doctorates or master's degrees in Christian theology and cognate disciplines could find work in places other than seminaries or theological colleges. Within a rather short time, that "market" for employment far surpassed the traditional seminary and other sources of gainful employment. So normative did it become for persons trained in the disciplines of Christian theology to look for work in secular or semi-secular institutions that many schools of theology found it necessary to change their degree nomenclature to suit the new labor market. Some decades ago, my own alma mater generously offered to transform my doctorate in theology (ThD) to one in philosophy (PhD). Fortunately, I was in a position to decline this offer. (Why should I exchange the most difficult degree to obtain at Union Seminary in the 1950s—one held, moreover, by the likes of Martin Luther—for a PhD, an amorphous degree that had in the meantime become commonplace?) But many of my contemporaries, needing or already holding jobs in institutions that hadn't the faintest idea what the letters *ThD* stood for (or, if they did, were innately suspicious of that designation), were glad to have themselves officially transformed into philosophers—free of charge, as I recall.

It is, of course, entirely possible to teach Christian theology in a secular institution, to do so with conviction, and to combine this work with a high degree of responsibility for the life and work of the church. In fact, that is what I have tried to do for the past three decades in the Faculty of Religious Studies of McGill University. Since I previously spent ten years as a seminary professor, I am able to compare the two categories with some knowledge of the possibilities and difficulties associated with each. It has been my good fortune to be a member of a university that, although a very secular one, has had a certain history of respect for Christianity and Christian theology. It was also to my advantage that I had been invited to that university on the basis of publishing and other activity in which I had already established my quite *confessional* approach to my discipline. My experience has convinced me, nonetheless, that it is possible in secular and pluralistic settings to combine a strong concern for academic excellence with an equally serious and manifest commitment to the welfare of the Christian movement. It can be done, and many have done it and are doing it.

But it cannot be done easily! Specifically, it cannot be done without a constant vigilance regarding the almost-inevitable tendency within the academy to become so conscious of one's position vis-à-vis the intellectual community, especially one's own professional "guild," that serious commitment to the community of faith comes to occupy a peripheral place in one's consciousness. Universities rarely reward people for writing books that can be understood by ordinary people or attending conferences and symposia unblessed by high-profile personages and dedicated to explicitly faith-based themes.

DEPRIVING THE CHURCH

The consequence of this double handicap to the vocation of theology—a church that has avoided theology and theologians, as well as a professional guild that wants to keep scholarship well above the commons—is that both professional theology and the churches have been deprived of the very thing that both need very badly, namely, mutuality of concern and dialogue. I have already indicated what this deprivation means for the theologian. He or she loses touch with what is the very essence of the concept of vocation, Christianly and biblically understood: its character as appointment *by* God *to* a community. Vocation becomes profession.

But it is the other partner in this essential dialogue that suffers most: the church. The academic world will not be much affected if even a large number of teaching theologians find their identity more with the academy than with the church. But the church will be—has been!—profoundly affected by the failure of so many of its teachers and potential teachers to exercise a serious and sustained vocation within it. And I mean a vocation *as theologians*, teachers, not only as people who "go to church."

What happens to the churches when they are abandoned by their teachers is hardly news. They become collectivities of a nebulous sort of "fellowship," or of random activism, or of undifferentiated "spirituality," or of moralisms old or new, or simply of "nice" people who don't quite know why they are there but feel they ought to be. Among the traditionally "high" churches, priests and parishioners tend to "escape into liturgy," as the Presbyterian theologian Arthur Cochrane used to put it. Periodically, churches deprived of critical theology are overtaken by urges and fads and programs inspired by the latest educational techniques or best-selling "religious" books in which, for instance, it is revealed that some are going to be "left be-hind" or that many of the things Christians believe are really just ancient lore and *mythos* found in many other places. For when the house has been swept clean of old devils (the oppressive orthodoxies of the past), seven new devils (or old ones in new disguises) enter in.

Theology will not save the churches! But if the churches continue to be as theology-poor—as thought-poor—as they are, they will either lack any commanding reasons to go on or disappear into a thousand sectarian factions, most of them driven by dogmatisms far more intrusive than any theology in its past "interference" in the life of the *ecclesia*.

Today, when the future of the Christian church in the Western world is fraught with uncertainty, there is a greater need for sound teaching than ever before in church history. Therefore, it is imperative for us to reclaim for ourselves the biblical and Reformation insistence upon theology as vocation. To do so will require *of the churches* that they overcome the adolescent's disease of rejecting every kind of authority in the name of a pseudodemocratic assumption that everybody is already theologically knowledgeable, just on the grounds of being human. Christianity is a historical faith; we are simply not born with the knowledge of it. "Are all teachers?" And of the theologians, it will require that they pay far less attention to the games that academics play and far more to the community of uncertain faith that nevertheless underwrites, directly and indirectly, their very inclusion in the academy.

SCOPE OF THIS BOOK

The following chapters develop, in a variety of ways, the perspective and concerns of this introduction. Chapter 1, "On Being a Christian Theologian," describes the theologian's life as being, on the one hand, accountable to a tradition that he or she did not devise—ergo "bound"—yet on the other hand responsible for a present and future testimony to the faith that cannot and must not be a mere repetition of *any* received tradition. I felt I had become "free" as a theologian only when I was able to realize that any truly worthy tradition by which I had felt bound had, in fact, just one great aim, so far as my own appropriation of it was concerned: to inculcate in me enough wisdom and courage to free me *from* false bondage, including bondage to itself, and *for* a grateful witness to the Word that God speaks here and now.

The second and longest chapter, this book's centerpiece, is a three-part study entitled "A Theologian's Journey." The journey in question is my own, and this chapter is a revised and somewhat expanded version of three talks that a thoughtful bishop of the Evangelical Lutheran Church in America asked me to prepare and deliver for the clergy of her synod. Later I gave the addresses in another form in Honolulu, and they were recorded at that time for television broadcast. I have retained the style of the lectures because I wished them to be "heard" in that form also by those reading them. There is something to be said for autobiographical reflection that attempts to speak quite directly to one's hearers or readers. Being a theologian is not, after all, an abstract, featureless, or emotionally neutral occupation. Theology is always done by specific persons, and Christian theology, when it is pursued deeply and seriously, positively evokes the personal in a way that few other pursuits of the mind do. Imagine: an individual human being essays to understand and speak of (*logos*) God (*theos*). Of God!—the "Eternal Thou" who addresses and would be addressed by our "I"

(Buber) in all the specificity of that term. One might well ask the question put to Job by the Voice out of the whirlwind: "Who is this that darkeneth counsel by words without knowledge?" (Job 38:2 KJV). Who *is* this who dares to undertake theology? How has it come about that this person feels inspired or compelled to take on such a grandiose (today one would have to say, I suppose, such an obsolete) role? What has gone into the mix of such a life? What strange ingredients have been blended there to produce such a strange ambition, indeed, such egregious presumption?

There was, of course, a time—and it was not long ago—when theology, like most other academic disciplines, strained to eliminate from its utterance any hint of the personal. Among the strictest sects of theological scribes, even the first-person singular was never used, except under syntactical duress. Happily, this bow to alleged scholarly detachment has almost disappeared from contemporary theological writing, and some honest and inventive present-day Christian writers have even developed the concept of theology *as* biography,[5] or vice versa. Perhaps that approach too has its inherent flaws; there is no nonproblematic theology! But it represents a refreshing change from the near subterfuge of many "classical" works of theology, whose seeming objectivity cloaks the actual, often highly manipulative subjectivity lurking behind the carefully chosen impersonal expressions. Augustine's *Confessions* have endured and intrigued others as long as they have precisely *because* the "I" who wrote them is present and real enough to make the "Thou" whom he addressed in them equally present and real.

The third chapter, "Stewards of the Mysteries of God: Preserving Classical Protestant Theology," applies the concept of vocation corporately to the remnants of mainstream Protestantism in North America and elsewhere today. Theologians claiming the Protestant heritage, whatever their particular ecclesiastical or doctrinal bent, are called to distinguish Reformation-based faith from a very great deal of what calls itself Protestantism in the global context today. The recently published *Encyclopedia of Protestantism*, in its article on statistics,[6] uses the nomenclature "core Protestantism" and "wider Protestantism" to tabulate the quantitative status of Protestantism worldwide. Almost gloating over the numerical growth of Protestantism in Africa, Asia, and Latin America, the authors of the article note, "The future of Protestantism may be found . . . outside of its European and American homelands." Its "cultural forms," they write, "may be largely unrecognizable to Western Protestants," though "its traditions and doctrines" *will remain intact.* Will they? That claim seems, in light of developments in the Anglican communion and elsewhere, presumptuous. Much of the religious climate in the "developing" world seems (according to reliable witnesses within those settings) a far cry from classical Protestantism. Indeed, much of the religious climate in the United States of America itself defies inclusion in Protestantism classically conceived! The very category of the encylopedists, "wider Protestantism," suggests Protestantism so *very* wide as to beg the question of its usefulness as a category. The encyclopedia quotes, and seems to approve of, the definition of *Protestant* in *Webster's New World Dictionary of the American Language*: "any Christian not belonging to the Roman Catholic or Orthodox eastern church"!

Clearly, Protestantism is badly in need of clarification. Unfortunately, liberal and moderate denominations in North America, the inheritors of the Protestant "mainstream," appear so demoralized, tentative, and cowed by the growth of "wider" Protestantism that they are failing conspicuously to represent the foundational principles of the Reformation and to distinguish them from "Protestant" aberrations.[7] The *political* functioning of such aberrant Protestantism makes this vocation of theology even more indispensable than if it were only a matter of doctrine. Unless the stewarding of classical Protestantism is assumed by its remnants in today's world, Protestantism is fated to become something vastly different from what the Reformers stood for. So far as its public image is concerned, I fear this has already occurred. I argue therefore that Protestant theologians in North America today have a common calling: to become "stewards of the mysteries of God" as these have been vouchsafed to us in the theological, ethical, and political heritage of the Reformation.

The fourth chapter, "Words," is a meditation on the challenge—not to say the great difficulty, not to say the impossibility—of "doing theology" in the first place. Anyone who thinks that theology is a placid, almost natural vocation for Christians, an enterprise full of blessed assurance and thus wonderfully free of the spiritual and intellectual struggle to which serious human thought is heir, has not yet been exposed to theological depth. Probably most of us who have felt theology to be our vocation have known ourselves covertly, if not openly, to be persons who do not "believe" easily! As Jürgen Moltmann has written, "We are not theologians because we are particularly religious; we are theologians because in the face of this world we miss God."[8] In addition to the difficulties created by our own ignorance and doubt, we are called to address a world in which God seems absent or silent. How do we speak of God in such a godless world (or, it may be, a world already too drunk on gods)? What words can be found to witness to God's ineffable and incarnate Word in an age that, with much justification, is notoriously distrustful of words? If we would define it on the grounds of the testimony of its greatest practitioners, then the vocation of theology, far from being the ladder to the professional prominence for which it has too often been pursued, might better be described as a form of spiritual suffering—hopefully, suffering "with Christ" (Rom 8:17).

The fifth and final chapter, "*De Profundis*: On Going 'Right Deep Down into Life,'"extends chapter 4's meditation on words, but it goes beyond the peculiarly linguistic aspect of the theological vocation and locates the intellectual challenge of this discipline— this discipleship—in the spiritual depths of the theologian's struggle with God. Real theology cannot be satisfied with mere storytelling, including the storytelling that passes for high academic scholarship, for at base it is about the most abysmal and never fully consummated relationship of one's earthly life: the relationship with that searching, truth-demanding, and inexplicably compassionate Thou in whose presence one falls forever short of becoming the I whom one is called to be.

CHAPTER ONE

On Being a Christian Theologian

Karl Barth, the theologian who most stimulated my earlier thought and writings, in his old age wrote some words that I find quite splendid:

> Theology . . . demands free people. As a young theologian, I belonged to a school. It was not a bad school. I still think of my teachers of that time with gratitude. But later I had to free myself from their school, not because much in their thinking was wrong, but simply because it was a school.[1]

This seemingly simple statement by a theologian who wrote more than anyone in the history of our faith, even Thomas Aquinas, contains a profound truth: one does not become a serious theologian until one has experienced the freedom to pursue the promptings of the divine Spirit without always looking over one's shoulder to see whether "the authorities" approve. By the authorities, I do not mean only, or even primarily, ecclesiastical authorities. I mean those sources of inspiration and wisdom that the fledgling thinker of theological thoughts has relied upon—authorities for whom one may still, like the old Barth, be truly grateful, but who must now recede into the background as one tries to come to terms with the great questions of faith and life in a personal, timely, and "original" way.

For me, that moment (which was, of course, more than just a moment) came in 1972–73, when I attempted my first large book.

It was a book in which I wanted to explore the ways in which the Christian message might address our own North American context, at the point where we seemed, as a culture, to be emerging from the naive optimism of our beginnings and finding ourselves confronted by all manner of negations for which we had no psychic or spiritual frame of reference. As I will explain in chapter 2, I wrote that book (*Lighten Our Darkness*) in Germany. One night during that time, on a trip to Switzerland, I wandered in the rain around the wonderful old cathedral of Basel, where Barth had lived and taught, and began mentally making a heartfelt speech to the great man: "Dear Karl Barth," I said, "I am terribly grateful to you—and to your one-time student Bonhoeffer, and to my teachers Reinhold Niebuhr and Paul Tillich and the others—for all that you have handed over to me. Without this, I could never have achieved the boldness to write such a book as I am now writing. But all the same, this evening I must advise you that I shall no longer rely as much on you and your generation of theologians—no longer seek your approval, no longer feel the need, even, to quote you constantly. No doubt I shall make mistakes as I venture forth on this new path—oh, how utterly presumptuous of me it is to attempt such a thing! Yet you yourself and the others have pushed me toward this moment; and I would certainly have failed to learn from you had this moment never arrived. *Herzlichen Dank, sehr geehrter Professor*, and—for the moment at least—*Auf Wiedersehen*. Perhaps we shall meet in heaven, and then you can tell me what you think of my ideas—that is, if you can drag yourself away from listening to those perpetual concerts of your great friend, W. A. Mozart!"

Well, in this quite homely way, I introduce to you my entirely serious theme. It is, as you see, about freedom. But it is about a special kind of freedom, a freedom that is not necessarily compatible with everything that calls itself freedom, especially in this sociological context of ours, whose every other word is precisely *freedom*. To the advocates of the vaunted freedom of America, theological freedom must seem a strange anomaly, for it presupposes something like bondage or at least adherence, including (yes!) respect for authority. Even more important, it is a freedom that—in the moment in which it is fully realized—entails a new and very demanding kind of responsibility.

LISTENING TO THE PAST

Let me say a little about each of these "bookends" of theological freedom—on the one side, listening to the past, and, on the other, responsibility to present and future. Being a Christian theologian means being bound to a narrative and commentary upon existence far transcendent of oneself. Christian theology is not the undertaking of an individual alone, not even of a cohort or generation of persons—a school. It is the undertaking of a community, a movement, a *communio viatorum*, a wayfaring fellowship that extends backward in time to those core events that shaped its beginnings—yes, and beyond even those uniquely revelatory events to the long history of the people whose remembrance and hope constitute the matrix without which the suffering and triumph of the Christ cannot be understood. To think theologically and to write theology, one must have served a kind of apprenticeship to that long tradition—an apprenticeship that, to be sure, never ends and that must especially occupy a good deal of time at the beginning, before one can branch out more or less on one's own.

I am speaking, of course, about tradition. From time to time, Christians, including alleged theologians, have imagined that they needed no tradition. You could do it yourself—a particularly appealing thought in our "New World." But the hoary history of these avowedly traditionless experiments proves the truth of the saying that those who do not remember the past are doomed to repeat it—replete with its most grievous mistakes.

In practice, to submit oneself to tradition means, of course, to pay attention to some particular tradition or traditions. Just as you cannot learn how to be a violinist without putting yourself under the tutelage of some particular violin teacher or school of violin playing (the Russian, the French, the Italian, or whatever), so it is with theology: You cannot simply submit yourself to "the Tradition." You have to open yourself to this or that *representation* of the great, diverse, multifaceted tradition of the Judeo-Christian past. Usually, this particular representation is not so much a matter of choice as it is of geography, heritage, and historical accident. Karl Barth was reared in a Reformed Swiss setting in the late nineteenth and early twentieth centuries; it would have been unusual had he fallen under the influence of any tradition other than Calvinist Protestantism and (given the later-nineteenth-century background) Reformed theology in its most liberal expressions.

This accidental factor in theological formation is not without its problems. As we all know, it easily and regularly happens that a dead traditional*ism* gradually emerges from a too intense and uncritical (even parochial) attachment to this or that specific living tradition. Today, in fact, we face the results of more than a millennium of this kind of misuse of tradition, so that Christianity's future depends in considerable measure upon unhitching exclusivistic communities of faith from a traditionalism they have mistaken for the tradition they did not learn well enough to know was only a means to a greater end.

That greater end is the same freedom that the old Barth spoke of when he said theology "demands free people." In fact, the test that should be applied to any tradition—*any*, including even the Bible—is whether it helps, in the end, to give birth to that freedom. This freedom, Christianly understood, presupposes the apprenticeship of Christian tradition; and that is no light matter. Karl Barth did not experience freedom in relation to the school to which he first belonged (liberal Protestant theology) until he had given himself to that school for a significant period of his life. And when I myself felt the time had come to say good-bye to old Karl and his cohort there in the damp shadows of Basel Cathedral, I had already been teaching theology for a decade or so. The true freedom possible in theology requires a significant degree of prior bondage. The substance of this discipline does not materialize simply out of our own entelechy. It is handed over (*tradere*) to us—and always in the form of specific interpretations of the mystery that no human words or symbols can fully contain. Yet the test of our authentic appropriation of the tradition remains whether it becomes the birth pangs of theological freedom. In sum, Christians are bound by a tradition whose goal, if we allow it, is to set us free.

RESPONSIBILITY TO PRESENT AND FUTURE

The other bookend of theological freedom is equally important. With that freedom comes an awesome new awareness of responsibility—and so, in a sense, another phase of bondage, a fresh accountability. Indeed, compared even with the rigorous attention and devotion required to acquaint oneself adequately with the Christian tradition, the discipline and maturity evoked by the actualization of this new theological freedom are infinitely more demanding. Paul Tillich, one of my most influential teachers, frequently used to speak of "theological courage." The term seemed strange to our young, North American ears, for we are accustomed in this society to associating courage with action, not thought. But I cannot say how often during my three or four decades as a writing theologian I have had occasion to remember that term: *theological courage*.

Just consider for a moment what is involved: the theologian is charged with the responsibility of interpreting for his or her own time and place the very core of the faith—gospel for the here and now. In the first place, this cannot be done without daring to think that one has really heard and understood the Christian message oneself, in all of its existential profundity—and that is already an immense assumption and risk!

In the second place, it cannot be done without daring to think that one has grasped, in some authentic sense, the character of one's own epoch, one's own *Sitz im Leben* or zeitgeist, one's own context or historical moment—and that is, if anything, an even greater risk. For who, living in the here and now, can truly say what it means to live in the here and now? Yet precisely this insight is a requirement of real theology. It is no theology that merely announces what was said and done in the past—what questions people asked in the Middle Ages, what answers theologians gave in the sixteenth century, or what concerns are held by Christians living in some other part of the world. Yes, theology has an indispensable historical component. But to become theology, not just historical doctrine or religious erudition, Christian thought must have been pierced to the heart by the pathos of the human condition *here* and *now*. Only by exposing ourselves to the often cruel and painful realities of the present, without the benefit of ready-made answers to everything, can we make good the claim to be theologians. And that is why Luther, the Catholic monk and Protestant theologian who, in my experience at least, most exemplifies what is meant by the responsibility that is given with this new freedom, said that theologians are made not just by reading and speculating, but by "living, dying and being damned."[2]

Not only for oneself must the theologian discern the signs of the times and determine how these can be engaged and changed by gospel; beyond that, the theologian must embrace such a vocation for the sake of others, for the sake of the church broadly conceived. The student I used to be—the young man who read Barth and listened to Niebuhr, Tillich, John Coleman Bennett, Paul Scherer, and those other great teachers with such enthusiasm; that still-young apprentice who, as a teacher of theology, continued to glory in the joys of learning from others what the Christian faith was all about—did not yet know how great is the courage demanded of those who actually write theology or dare to speak publicly as if they understand this discipline. For then, with the freedom and inner compulsion that is presupposed by the vocation to write, comes the realization that what one writes will actually be read—by some, at least. And some will take it seriously. Some will actually believe it! Some will make what for them are momentous decisions under the impact, in part, of what one says. And then what?

Does one dare to be that audacious? Sometimes, over these past two or three decades, I have met people—young and old, students, clergy, laity—who have told me that this or that piece I had written, this or that book or essay, had been terribly important for them. While I have been humanly touched, I often have felt like saying to them in all honesty, "Yes, but be careful! I am just a human being, 'prone to evil and slothful in good,' as the ancient prayer of confession says, as well as highly fallible intellectually." Thus, in the latter years of my full-time teaching, I frequently took to uttering a line that usually brought a laugh from my students (but I hope it also brought some kind of self-knowledge into their own thinking and preaching): "In theology one has to keep talking, because otherwise somebody will believe your last sentence."

The point is that theologians, like Christians in general, must live with and seek to articulate Truth—*living* Truth that only rarely can even be glimpsed and never, ever fully captured in concepts and words. And theologians must do this as those who would be teachers of others, guides for the church in its uncertain voyage on the dark waters of time, witnesses to Good News in a world that staggers from one piece of bad news to the next. The theological vocation, then, requires a courage that is more than natural—the courage of being, in Paul's language, a "fool for Christ," a courage that darkly suspects, however, that most of the time it is just playing the fool.

PRIVILEGE AND JOY

Bound, free, responsibility, courage—these words belong to the calling of the theologian. But lest such words convey too great a heaviness, I will conclude by conjuring up two other words that also most certainly belong to this vocation: *privilege* and *joy*.

Sometime in the 1980s, I was on a flight bound for California, where I was to give some long-forgotten lectures at some long-forgotten event. By a fluke, I had been bumped up into first class, and I sat there in all that unaccustomed luxury, ready to relax and prepare myself for the event in question. Beside me (or rather, in the next seat over, for to those accustomed to the cramped conditions of economy, the next seat in first class seems wondrously far away) sat an important-looking gentleman in a three-piece suit, studying some papers that appeared enormously decisive. I was rather pleased that he seemed absorbed in his study of these documents, because when you have to talk a good deal at the end of your voyage, you need (at least I do) to enjoy as much Benedictine silence as possible on the way there.

The grave gentlemen soon, however, gave every indication (alas!) of desiring human discourse, so, as a defense, I asked him questions about himself—questions requiring, it seemed, lengthy responses. He was, he told me, an executive officer of a large firm (IBM, I think). He went into some detail about this and then (a moment I dreaded but knew was inevitable) said to me, "And what do *you* do?"

Now, I must tell you that usually when this question is put to me en route, I—well, I lie. I sometimes say I am a teacher of philosophy or of literature, subjects about which I do at least know a little. I do not lie out of sheer perversity but because, when you tell the truth about your profession, if you are a minister or anything like that, your partner in conversation immediately hides himself or herself in more or less pious talk. And if there is any value at all in conversations while traveling, it is the value of a certain rare truth telling ("What does it matter? I'll never see him again"). However, the gentleman in the adjoining seat seemed earnest, and it was a long, long flight, so I decided to be truthful myself for a change and said straight out, "I am a theologian," fully expecting that this would bring an effective end to any genuine discussion.

"Oh," said my fellow traveler enthusiastically, "now tell me about that. What *is* theology? What do you actually . . . do?"

Well, we had two or three more hours to go, so I thought, "Why not try to give him a decent answer?" I talked nonstop then for about twenty minutes. At the end of this oration in the skies, my seat partner turned to me and said, in what seemed the most earnest manner, "My, it must be wonderful *to think about everything all the time.*" His very words!

For a moment, I thought that he was mocking me. But his face and the sentences that gushed out of him afterward confirmed his entire sincerity. "I used to think about everything, too," he confessed. "I even prayed! But now I am just tied to this cursed, confining world of business!"

How often I have wished that I had a verbatim record of the answer that I gave to that man's questions, "What is theology? What does a theologian actually do?" Because his response to my little lecture on the subject is precisely the response I should always like to evoke: "How wonderful—to think about everything all the time!"

Surely, to be a Christian theologian really is to open oneself—or, more accurately, to find oneself *being opened*—to everything: every testimony to transcendence, every thought and experience of the human species, every wonder of the natural order, every reminiscence of the history of the planet, every work of art or literature, every motion picture, every object of beauty and pathos—everything under the sun, and the sun, too! Nothing is excluded a priori, nothing forbidden, nothing foreign. One need not be bound by external factors, nor even by internal factors, such as the need to be always consistent with what one has already perceived to be true. I love Saint Augustine because he was in some important things consistent, but I love him even more because he changed—when the divine Spirit and the spirit of the times made change more mandatory than consistency.

And it *is* "wonderful" to be free in that way, because (as my businessman seat partner rightly discerned) that kind of openness belongs in some inalienable way to the human condition at its best. Theologians are certainly not the only people who may experience such spiritual expansiveness, and, by the same token, let us admit that many theologians do not. Most of the time, most of us do not. But it remains true, all the same, what the old Karl Barth wrote at the end of a long life of disciplined and demanding theological work: "Theology demands free people."

I began by quoting a great Protestant named Karl; I shall end by quoting a great Roman Catholic Karl—Karl Rahner, who in this lovely statement says somewhat differently the same thing as Karl Barth:

> It is the bitter grief of theology and its blessed task, too, always to have to seek (because it does not have present to it at the time) what in a true sense—in its historical memory—it has always known . . . always providing that one has the courage to ask questions, to be dissatisfied, to think with the mind and heart one actually has, and not with the mind and heart one is supposed to have.[3]

CHAPTER TWO

A Theologian's Journey

As for me, I regard myself as a Christian.

–Martin Luther

As is well known, old men tell stories. The cynic may say they do so because they can't do much else. There is an element of truth in this. Nevertheless, old men have another reason for telling stories. In, say, seventy-six years (my present age), a human being accumulates many megabytes of history. If he or she is half alive and half observant, an older person's memory is fairly crammed with words, events, experiences, sense and nonsense. I love the verse at the conclusion of John's gospel where, summing up his attempts at a mini-biography of Jesus, the author sort of throws up his hands and declares, "But there are also many other things which Jesus did; were every one of them to be written, I suppose that the world itself could not contain the books that would be written" (John 21:25 RSV). And Jesus only lived until his mid-thirties!

For the past two summers, in a leisurely way that I had almost forgotten how to practice, I did something I had been threatening to do ever since I attained the biblical age: I began to write an autobiography—not for publication, just for myself. A friend told me that it was a terribly egotistical thing to do, and I suppose it is. But I thought to myself, "Listen, if you have been granted all those years (a thing neither your father nor his father was granted—they died at forty-five and fifty-six, respectively), then you are under some kind of obligation to life to think about it in a sustained and serious way." "The unexamined life," as the more-than-seventy-years-of-age Socrates said, "is not worth living."[1] In any case, I felt the need to reflect on my sojourn through time. I do not have the skill of my onetime fellow student Frederick Buechner, who has done this for his grateful public, but in the process of writing those summertime reflections on my life, I found myself increasingly caught up in an absorbing exercise in remembrance. I have written more than six hundred pages so far, and there is still a third of my life to account for. So many stories.

And so many changes. At every turn in my reflections and jottings, I had cause to meditate on the unprecedentedly changeful character of the period of Western history with which my life has coincided. In 1928, the year I was born, we had still not become the city dwellers we are today (80 percent of Canadians now live in cities). Villages like the village of my childhood and adolescence were still not bedroom communities for nearby cities; they had a distinctive and remarkably independent culture of their own. My grandparents, farmers on both sides, still worked their farms with horses, milked their cows by hand, and were only just beginning (with misgivings) to get electricity and party-line telephones. Only a few people owned cars. A very small percentage of young people ever anticipated going to university, and in the universities there were many excellent teachers who had never acquired PhDs and felt no compulsion to do so. People's homes, before the age of ubiquitous advertising, were not duplicates of one another. The horror of World War I (which we called "the Great War") was still very much in the air, but even if we didn't buy into the eternal-peace rhetoric of the idealists, we certainly hadn't yet learned to consider war a permanent and prominent feature of human existence. The movies we saw—rarely, at least among my sort—were naive, both in the sense of being simplistic (good guys/bad guys) and in terms of a certain lovely innocence for which today many oldsters (I, too) periodically feel rather nostalgic.

If you have a lot of other information, one statistic in its way tells the story: in 1928 only two billion human beings inhabited planet Earth. During my lifetime, the population of the world has tripled. Individuals who are disciplined and imaginative enough to acquire the necessary information and insight to research the past can, of course, learn a great deal about this period of "rapid social change," as it has been called. But to have lived through it is to have stored up feelings that cannot be acquired, sights that cannot be reproduced even by the best photography, smells that no longer linger among us, hopes and fears and ways of regarding time itself that are lost to the present. And it is also, I suspect, to feel a vague but undeniable rootlessness, as though one were a kind of displaced person, an alien in one's own homeland. Yes, this too—this primal lostness and melancholy—can be noticed by the observant as a quality of the seventy-, eighty-, and ninety-year-olds of our concrete cities and our standardized kitchens and bathrooms. Our disorientation is not due only to age; it's because so much of what we called home has mysteriously disappeared.

Yet, despite the nostalgia and even the periodic sorrow that characterizes all honest autobiography today, the most compelling mood engendered by my own exercise in remembering has not been melancholy. To the contrary, the exercise has given me something like a new lease on life—even new *hope*, thus demonstrating the truth of Paul Ricoeur's contention that, in the end, remembrance and hope are the same thing. For what I have learned through this exercise, above all, is that there has been a great deal in my life for which the only appropriate response would be gratitude. If you look at your life day by day, year by year, even decade by decade, you are apt to be conscious of all the problems, all the little anxieties, all the perils that lurk around the corner, waiting to pounce. But if you try to get an overview of your sojourn—preferably from a perspective of several decades—you often are able to draw quite different conclusions. I have certainly not been happy every day of my life; I am not that sort, not a native optimist! But I have found, through this act of memory, that the big picture presents a surprising and wholly uncalculated affirmation of life.

If the first lesson in my autobiographical attempt was to convince me that I'd enjoyed an undeservedly meaningful existence, the second was even more illuminating: it was that I owe such happiness as I have had to one Source—namely, the sheer grace of God *as it is mediated through the lives of other people.* I had set out to write about my own life, but what I discovered through the plain task of chrono-logically recounting my own story was that most of the time, I was actually writing about other people. That alone would have justified the entire exercise. It is wonderful and illuminating to realize (and it is never too late to do so) that one's life from the very beginning and throughout the years has been a gift from others, continuously given—others both immediately present and distant, both contem-poraries and persons dead for centuries, both intimate and remote from one's day-to-day existence. I will tell you about some of these others—my teachers, the historical thinkers who influenced me through their writings, and a few of my close contemporaries. But I will not name most of those who have given me the needed imagi-nation and courage and zest for life. You would not recognize their names, for they are not public figures but ordinary folk—old ladies and gentlemen of my youth, people in the various workplaces of my life, members of my one and only congregation, and, of course, my students and colleagues of more than four decades in academic life. Most of these people did not know they were giving me gifts of in-sight and support, affirmation and critical acumen, but were simply being who they were and doing what they do.

This, too, is an important lesson to learn, preferably *before* you reach the age of seventy-six. Every one of us plays the role of giver, wittingly or unwittingly, in relation to all whom we meet. And if we know this about ourselves, we may be inspired to pay a good deal more attention than otherwise to the way that we are with one another, the things we say to one another, the deeds we do and leave undone.

I will concentrate on the professional side of my pilgrimage, though I don't think you would want me to leave out the personal altogether. I couldn't, actually, for my journey as a theologian *is* a personal story. Yet it is not a merely private one. For I have been part of a generation. I inherited from my teachers—and I was blessed to have as teachers many of the great theologians of the immediate past—most of what I know. And I have shared very common influ-ences and experiences with my own cohort of Christian theologians and scholars (including friends like Walter Brueggemann, Phyllis Trible, Jürgen Moltmann, Kosuke Koyama, Barbara Brown Taylor, Gregory Baum, and many others). By now, I have been a participating witness in many changes in social, religious, and ecclesiastical self-understanding, some of them watershed changes. I've been through a whole gamut of "theologies *of*": the theology of crisis, the theology of secularity, the theology of hope, the theology of liberation, feminist theologies, and many others.

In short, I have not been alone. How could I be alone—in the church? So, while the story I am going to tell you here is certainly my story, and I do not want to blame anybody else for the way it is told, it is also the story of an era. It is therefore, in some way, your story, too. Some of you, who are closer to my generation, will be able to identify with a good deal of it, I suspect. For the younger people, it may not be so immediate—at least in the story of my past; yet I hope that through your historical and other studies, you fifty-year-old youngsters and others will find plenty of points of contact even with this first part, "Where I Have Been."

Where I Have Been

"Where I have been" is, in fact, a pretty long and complex story, so I shall not be able to elaborate at great length on any of its phases. It will be rather episodic—postmodern, if you like. But it should not be just confusing, so I'll try to guide you with subheads.

BEGINNINGS

In 1953, at age twenty-five, I went down to New York City to begin my theological studies at Union Theological Seminary. Senator McCarthy's anticommunist witch hunt was in full swing, and many celebrated Americans and others were chanting the mantra "I am not a communist, I have never been a communist," and so on. In view of what I shall say presently about the earliest influences on my theological development, let me say straightaway that "No, I am not a Lutheran; I have never been a Lutheran; I do not intend to become a Lutheran." In fact, I have no Lutheran blood whatsoever, whether German or Scandinavian. I am strictly a WASP with a small, saving injection—some five generations ago—of Mohawk genes.[2]

All the same, my real awakening to the depths of the Christian faith is indelibly associated with the name of Martin Luther. I suppose I could echo the sentiments of my celebrated teacher, the church historian Wilhelm Pauck. One day an impertinent student asked him, "But where, Dr. Pauck, do *you* stand—personally?" And the puckish Pauck replied with a grin, "I have one foot in the Reformation and the other on a banana peel." The banana peel, for Pauck as for myself, is the ongoing and always unpredictable present, with its new and unsettling questions, its problems and possibilities: the moving edge of time, for which no tradition can wholly prepare one. Later, in the section "The Journey Ahead," I will draw heavily on the banana peel side of this dialectic.

Yet tradition—as the wonderful musical *Fiddler on the Roof* insists—is absolutely necessary for facing present and future, and some traditions are better at providing the wherewithal necessary to that task than are others. For me, Luther has been a particularly important exemplar and guide. In the next section, I shall explain in some detail why that is the case. For now it is enough to say that my real awakening to the depths of Christian faith began with my introduction to that Reformer.

I grew up in the church, as nearly everyone did at that time in my southwestern Ontario village. But apart from the Bible, which in those far-off days children and even young men in their twenties and thirties were actually expected to read and study in Sunday school—apart, I say, from that "strange new world within the Bible" (as Karl Barth called it),[3] I fear I found little of depth in the Christianity to which my village church introduced me. Even though I sensed great spiritual authenticity in some of the individuals in the congregation, I did not find in the church as a whole anything extraordinary, anything different or more gripping, really, from the village culture at large. What the church seemed chiefly to stand for was morality—indeed, a quite restrictive morality, as it was then. Such a religion could hold neither me nor my more independent friends beyond adolescence, though most of my contemporaries eventually made some kind of compromise with it.[4]

Then, through the influence of three clergymen of my denomination who really were different,[5] I stumbled onto Luther. In quick succession, at age twenty-one, I read three big biographies of the Reformer and a compendium of his writings. I felt at home at once. Luther's dismissal of "works righteousness," his explanation of "justification by grace through faith," his freedom from literalistic biblicism, and his irreverent and sometimes even scatological language charmed me entirely. I read of his journey of faith up to the Diet of Worms as though I were reading, in some other epoch and mode, my own spiritual autobiography. Without any previous knowledge of Luther (in my church, Wesley was quoted and sometimes Calvin, but never Luther), the young Luther seemed to me to have anticipated all my doubts, shared them, and found a way of living with them—and beyond them. He didn't ask me to be a "nice boy." He asked me to be truthful, to be myself, to *accept* myself despite all that was truly unacceptable about me. To trust!

Let me say that I never thought of Luther as heroic—only human, wonderfully, unconstrainably human. So I was not shocked when, later on, I found out about his clay feet—the feet he so frequently stuck into his big Saxonian mouth. But I would not have become a theologian (perhaps I would not have remained a Christian in any real sense of the word) had I not been introduced to this splendid, bombastic, impulsive, and deeply honest human being. Lutherans often have made poor Martin too heroic, too saintly. Perhaps they are embarrassed about the all-too-human side of the man. Christians are usually embarrassed about the all-too-human side of Jesus, too, so we end up with a Divinity incapable of real incarnation. Luther's famous Christmas sermon,[6] where he says that he would not have his hearers contemplate the infant Christ's "divinity" ("Divinity can crush a person," he says), but his humanity ("just as we see it in our own babies"): this could be applied to Luther himself. We should see him in all his errant and remarkable flesh-and-bloodness. It was the sheer humanity of his story and of his writing that made me think, "This kind of Christian seems to me *believable*. If I stick with the likes of him, I shall not be tempted to think"—as I had often done—"that Christianity is just a kind of wishful thinking, not to say pretense, that people adopt for the purposes of maintaining a good public image. Perhaps it is possible, after all, to be a Christian and to be a doubter, a skeptic, a questioner of all sorts of pretensions to finality. Perhaps one can be Christian and also oneself!"[7]

NEOORTHODOXY

A few years ago, I wrote a book about the so-called neoorthodox theologians, namely, the great Protestant theologians of the first fifty or sixty years of the twentieth century: Karl Barth, Paul Tillich, Reinhold and H. Richard Niebuhr, Emil Brunner, Dietrich Bonhoeffer, Suzanne de Dietrich, and others.[8] I called the book *Remembered Voices* because, for me, many of those voices were and are quite literally "remembered." They still perch on my shoulder and whisper things to me as I write. Sometimes they say encouraging things, sometimes not. But I know that I shall never be free of them, nor do I wish to be (though, as I have already indicated in chapter 1, neither do I feel bound to them; they'd be the first to deny me that!). The voices of Reinhold Niebuhr, Paul Tillich, John Coleman Bennett, and Paul Scherer are all immediately familiar: they were my teachers for several years. Karl Barth's voice is less familiar, though I sat in awe as I listened to him in 1962 in the Rockefeller Chapel at the University of Chicago, where he lectured for an entire week on evangelical theology.[9] And the voice of Dietrich Bonhoeffer, which, of course, I never literally heard (nor did many of the now living), has been for me, perhaps, the most insistent of all those "remembered voices."

Bonhoeffer's *The Cost of Discipleship* was the first strictly theological book that I ever read.[10] That was in the summer of 1949. The book had only just appeared in English. Only a handful of people in the English-speaking world, and few enough in Germany, had ever heard this name. I had just finished reading all that Luther, and here was an obviously serious and brilliant young German Lutheran warning all admirers of Luther, "Please, do not turn that splendid Reformation teaching about justification by grace into a principle! Do not make grace 'cheap.'"

I was enthralled by Bonhoeffer from the outset. But I did not fully understand his odd combination of piety and critical theology until I had lived a lot longer and got to know his Germany firsthand. Today I would say that if you want to comprehend this complex thinker, you have to know his sociohistorical context better than most North Americans do. And you should read his *Cost of Discipleship* and other earlier works in the light of his final thoughts, as they are collected in his *Letters and Papers from Prison*.[11] Bonhoeffer had such profound respect for Christian *faith* that he had finally to be extremely critical of the Christian *religion*. He had seen the reductio ad absurdum of imperial Christianity in his church's willingness to accept and absorb the racist nationalism of his country's Nazi leadership.

I had the great good fortune of studying at Union Theological Seminary for seven full years (1953–60). I had gone down there, after completing my BA at the University of Western Ontario in London, with the intention of staying for one year—and stayed for seven. Where else, at that time, would one want to go? They were arguably Union Seminary's best years. Not only in theology and ethics, where Tillich and Niebuhr were the best-known names, but in every field of theological investigation, there were scholars of the highest rank: James Muilenberg and Samuel Terrien in Old Testament; John Knox, J. Christiaan Beker, and Frederick Grant in New Testament; Arthur Jeffries and John Nock in comparative studies; Cyril Richardson, Robert Handy, and Wilhelm Pauck in church history; Henry Pitney Van Dusen, Robert McAfee Brown, David Roberts, Richard Kroner—the list goes on. Once (it was at Wartburg Seminary in Dubuque) when I was just beginning to lecture abroad, the person introducing me simply listed off the names of my teachers and then said, "If, with such mentors, a guy cannot do *something* worthwhile, what hope is there?"

I have always felt it was providential that when I was a student of these remarkable teachers, I was profoundly under the spell of Karl Barth, the Swiss Reformed theologian who wrote more than anyone else in the history of Christianity[12] and who said of himself that he himself was *not* "a Barthian," for he was far too creative a mind to be locked into a system, especially not one of his own devising (a thing that many who call themselves Barthians have not yet understood).[13] Under the spell of this giant from Basel, I sat in Tillich's classes, arguing with him all the while—silently, of course (we're not yet talking about the crass sixties!). Tillich was a Protestant apologist, and in what was then my frame of mind, I felt he was too accommodating to culture, to "the world." As a result of this ongoing silent but fervent argumentation with my great teacher, I learned far more from him than I was able to recognize at the time. But in the early sixties, when I began to teach theology myself, I realized how much I was indebted to Tillich. I saw that, to be the teacher of these students, I had to take with utter seriousness the actual situation in which they were living: that is, I had to apply what Tillich called "the method of correlation," co-relating Christian "answers" with the human question, simply in order to communicate with my students. The late Robert McAfee Brown once remarked that he had the same experience.

Barth helps to clarify the substance of the faith, but one needs Tillich to help communicate it. I can fairly say, then, in terms of my basic theological formation, that I am an odd combination of the teaching of the most kerygmatic and the most apologetic Protestant theologians of the past century: Barth, for whom God is "wholly other," and Tillich, for whom God is the Stranger one has already met. I still find myself moving between a Barthian emphasis on the otherness of God and the gospel and a Tillichian emphasis on the Christian message as one that meets and answers the human situation. I suppose that makes me, in fact, a disciple chiefly of Reinhold Niebuhr! For Niebuhr combined these two emphases creatively and with exquisite concreteness. Moreover, unlike Barth and Tillich, Niebuhr did this as a North American Christian and not, like Tillich, a European transplant.

Neoorthodoxy (and I am using this term broadly here; it is not a very satisfactory term, and its most vociferous representatives today usually betray it by making it nothing more than a resurgence of old-fashioned Protestant orthodoxy),[14] this critical theology that emerged in the midst of the two world wars and their aftermath, did something for me—for my whole generation, I would say—that must be done for every age of the church: it tried to think the faith *whole*, and to do so for the sake of the church. It was not first an academic theology, even in its most academic expressions; it was a theology for the Christian community. Barth was particularly clear about that. That is why he called his great work *Church Dogmatics*. But even Tillich, who among the theologians of this category was most concerned for the communication of the faith to the world, did most of his work with the Christian community in mind. He did not want to bypass the church in favor of a merely intellectual interest in "religion," though some of his followers did so. Moreover, particularly in his *Systematic Theology*, though not exclusively there, he tried to account for the whole tradition.[15] He took seriously the medieval assumption that "truth is one," so he tried to help us see, once again, the complex interrelatedness of all the doctrines, including doctrines that in many cases theological liberals of the nineteenth and early twentieth centuries had cast aside.

It is this emphasis upon the whole tradition—not an easy acceptance of it, but a determination to dialogue with the whole of it—that got lost after about 1960. Along with that went the assumption that theology has a special responsibility to the churches.[16]

THE SIXTIES

The year 1960 was a watershed year for me personally: I left the seminary (finally), got married (the best thing I ever did), and became a parish minister in a very small northern Ontario town, about four thousand people, at the top of Lake Huron, a lumbering town called by the unlikely name Blind River. After seven years in New York, I found that it was a long way from Broadway to Blind River. It took me several months to realize that I was expected to smile at people on the street. But I loved my parish of the United Church of Canada,[17] and I would gladly have remained much longer than the two years that we had there, but my denomination called me to become the first principal of a new college it was establishing in a new and burgeoning secular university in southwestern Ontario, the University of Waterloo. As a result, the little church in Blind River was and remains my one and only parish. From 1962 onward, my life unfolded in the context of the academic world.

The sixties (including the early 1970s) were a remarkable time by anybody's standard of measurement: wonderful, alluring, absurd, naive—in retrospect, even in some respects rather embarrassing. I think we all went a little mad. We fancied ourselves revolutionaries—and became in time, some of us, staid and successful middle-class types! We were inflamed by causes. Some of us were self-styled Marxists, some bohemians or hippies, and some impossible admixtures of the two. Suddenly, professors, like other alleged authority figures, became the brunt of frontal attacks that were often crude and cruel. On both sides of the Atlantic, students asserted their alleged rights. They didn't intend to be only listeners now; they intended to participate, and prominently—whether or not they knew anything about the subject in question. Professors who wanted to be popular (or perhaps even just to survive) showed up in jeans, sat on the desk and swung their legs, and cooed, "What shall we talk about today?"

I became a professor of theology in the midst of all that! In 1965, I was appointed to the MacDougald Chair of Systematic Theology in St. Andrew's College, University of Saskatchewan, in the beautiful western Canadian city of Saskatoon. I occupied this chair for ten years. Throughout that period, I never succumbed to the what-shall-we-talk-about-today approach. I prepared every lecture carefully and usually read from a manuscript, as many of my own teachers had done. I do not regret this, though it was often difficult.[18] I felt, as Günter Grass once put it, that in a wild, Dionysian time (then especially!) it is necessary for the prudent to be Apollonian, thoughtful, reasonable. Chaos may be creative, but it can also be destructive and demeaning, as Luther found out when he had to deal with the radicals of his own movement.

All the same, the chaos of the 1960s and early seventies was a necessary and, in the end, a salutary phase in Christian self-understanding on this continent. During that time, voices began to be heard that had not been heard before: African American/Canadian voices, the voices of women, of gays and lesbians, of indigenous peoples, of ethnic minorities. Also, the voices of thoughtful persons inside and on the edges of the churches, who could no longer be satisfied with the conventional doctrines and preaching of Christendom—people who were conscious of the growing secularism of our Western world and were not ready to see the Christian faith identified with its own most reactionary elements, but wished to recover its essence and make it accessible to their postreligious contemporaries. I am thinking of people like Harvey Cox, J. C. Hoekendijk, Leslie Newbigin, and—to a certain extent, but with reservations—the so-called death-of-God theologians. Above all, I think of J. A. T. Robinson.

Bishop Robinson's little book *Honest to God*,[19] the first of a series of popular, critical books by this theologian, previously well known as a New Testament scholar, was perhaps the most important religious publishing event of the 1960s. The book first appeared in 1963, and in 2002 Westminster John Knox Press published a fortieth-anniversary edition, for which I was asked to write one of the two extended introductions (the other is written by the present Archbishop of Canterbury, Rowan Williams).[20] So I read *Honest to God* again quite recently, as well as most of the other literature surrounding the whole debate that it sparked. Unlike my first reading of it forty years ago, this time I found it a surprisingly sober and responsible statement. In 1963, people felt (I, too, somewhat) that the bishop had gone too far. But if you read it today, realizing how far in the meantime the whole world and the whole church have gone, you are bound to consider *Honest to God* remarkably restrained. By comparison with Bishop John Spong's work, Robinson's approach is almost conservative. The whole aim of the Bishop of Woolwich was to conserve the essence of the faith as he understood it and to prevent its further erosion by a ubiquitous, one-dimensional secularity *as well as* its reduction to absurdity through co-optation by the literalist, biblicist elements within the churches. Considering the prominence that the latter element has acquired in the United States in the meantime, one wishes that *Honest to God* had been even more widely read than it was!

All these voices—the voices of the excluded, marginalized, and oppressed and the voices of thinking Christians like Robinson—were legitimized by the new openness that began to appear in the 1960s. They have since attained an irrevocable place in the life of the Christian community. Today it would be unthinkable for a serious theologian or minister of the historic "main line" to treat any area of doctrine (anthropology, for instance) or any scriptural text (for instance, Jesus' meeting with the Syrophoenician woman) as though such doctrines and texts were to be interpreted only by white, middle-class, male intellectuals. The critique coming from these formerly excluded voices has certainly not been fully absorbed or heeded, even by the mainline Protestant churches; but all the churches have been challenged if not changed by their critique.

Transitions as far-reaching as those introduced by the chaos (perhaps we can call it the "creative chaos," to borrow a favorite term of

Tillich) of the 1960s never occur, however, without some significant losses. Some of the things that were lost ought to have been lost long before, and we can say good riddance to them. Personally, I have no desire at all to go back to the smug, success-oriented churchianity of the 1950s. Too much of it, alas, still exists!

But there were unfortunate losses, too. The folksiness and so-called informality, the anything-goes one-dimensionality that replaced the middle-class propriety of the 1950s, does not seem to me an unquestionable gain. Didn't we do a flip-flop on that one? Didn't we rush too quickly into a television-inspired performance mode? It is not only older people who ask, "Whatever became of reverence?" Sometimes when I sit in church services, I think, "They were right, those death-of-God people. God really is dead, and we're all here trying to entertain one another in God's absence. Unfortunately, it's not very good entertainment."

At a deeper level of theological concern, I return to the observation that what the so-called neoorthodox theologians did for the church was to put it in touch with the whole tradition again, after the rather wild ultraliberal winnowing of the nineteenth century. That concern for the whole got lost during and after the 1960s, as moderate and liberal churches gave themselves more and more to cause-based and identity-based theologies.[21] Do not mistake me: We'd have been greatly impoverished without the introduction into the midst of Christian discourse of neglected ethical causes and marginalized identities. Yet it seems unfortunate that the immediacy and fervor of the many critical movements that began to be heard after 1960 pushed into the background the profound wrestling with the Christian faith that had occurred between 1910 and 1960. That fifty-year period represents, surely, one of the most creative and gripping moments in the entire evolution of Christian thought. Unfortunately, it did not filter down to the churches.

I say unfortunately, not only because I think theology is always important in and for the church; it cannot and must not remain a merely professional enterprise undertaken by people like me. But it was particularly unfortunate that so little of the work done by Barth, Brunner, Bultmann, the Niebuhr brothers and their sister

Hulda, Tillich, Suzanne de Dietrich, Dorothy Sayers, Bonhoeffer, and many others did not get a chance to enter the stream of ordinary Christian dialogue at that time. That must be considered a loss because at that time, and still today, the only thing that will prevent the churches, in the midst of their cultural and social disestablishment, from disintegrating or being taken over by very questionable, one-sided elements within them is a lively and deep *theological* renewal that includes but also transcends the many and varied voices and concerns of specific groups within the churches. The excitement of the various protesting theologies that came to the fore after 1960 tended to distract the churches from this more comprehensive theological task. To be sure, we can still hear, now and then, the names of the giants of the immediate past; but very few even of the clergy still read them or ponder the meaning of their deep and original struggle with the whole tradition.

THE TWILIGHT ZONE

The sixties were chaotic, but they were also permeated by a kind of euphoria (assisted, in some cases, chemically). *The Greening of America, The Making of a Counterculture*, the novels of Hermann Hesse—such books, accompanied by films and novels of a similar hue, expressed a mood of expectancy. There was a lot to be angry about or scared of: Vietnam, the Cold War, the breakdown of institutions (Watergate), the establishment's sometimes violent attack on protesting movements (Kent State), the deterioration of the environment (Rachel Carson), and so on. But we were also (to use a current expression) turned on by the fact that so many of us were *noticing* all that, being angry publicly, protesting, writing, and making films about it. There was hope in our sense of awakening, our determination to name what was wrong and to change it. Youth—"with a little help from its friends"—could make a new world!

It is not a little ironic, looking back, that while so much of the protest of that period directed itself against Middle America, it was at its core a resurgence of the American Dream—which is, of course, a version (the most concrete version) of the "modern" dream, the dream prepared by the Enlightenment of the eighteenth century, energized by the Romantic movements of the nineteenth century, and mechanized for use by the technological revolution of the twentieth century. After about 1975, perhaps 1980, that dream began once more to fade. We entered the twilight zone here in North America, as many Europeans had done much earlier.

We were wholly unprepared for it. We are still unprepared for it. We are still dismayed by the reality of evil, death, and the demonic. They just shouldn't be! They are not part of "the Plan"! And we are even more dismayed at the fact that evil, death, and the demonic are not just "out there"—among the communists (whom we can hardly blame anymore) or the terrorists (who have become the new enemy we've been waiting for). We've had to face the intimations of evil within ourselves: ourselves as individuals; ourselves as a society, ourselves as the epicenter of the power, wealth, and technological/military clout of the planet. The self-knowledge of America that brought Vietnam to an end may—in the light of the present dishonorable revelations concerning the lies that were told to justify the Iraq war, the treatment of Iraqi prisoners, and similar embarrassments—bring that unfortunate episode in the so-called war on terrorism to an end. Or perhaps one should say instead that such revelations may cause more of us to feel that "war" is an inappropriate response to the phenomenon *we* are calling terrorism.

I am writing this, as we write everything now, in the wake of September 11, 2001. As a Christian and a Canadian, I share with all of U.S. Americans a remembered sense of the horror of that event. Nothing at all, I suspect, has been accomplished by those appalling acts of violence—nothing but still more and greater violence. Yet, in the intervening years, I have heard far too little profound reflection on this continent upon the symbolic significance of these attacks: namely, that they were aimed precisely at the centers of greatest economic and military-technical power on earth. Many Americans still ask, "Why do they hate us so? We are nice people!" And, as a Canadian who knows the United States rather well, let me say to any who doubt it, they are! U.S. Americans as a people are the nicest, most hospitable, most generous people in the world. But America is also empire, much as Americans hate to admit it. Empires have never been liked. The British Empire, in whose bosom I spent my childhood, was thoroughly hated throughout the world. So was the Roman Empire. We possessing peoples of the Northern Hemisphere are naive about the alienating spin-off of our own conspicuous power and prosperity. Whether we like it or not, for very large segments of this world, "America" (with its satellites) is "the evil empire"—and today the only remaining candidate for that rather nasty distinction. It is, of course, an exaggerated and even a ridiculous way of thinking. Christians know that the demonic, like the divine, transcends all human beings and institutions. But, as Reinhold Niebuhr and Martin Luther King Jr. and most of the greatest prophets and artists of the United States have warned us all, we North Americans shall have to become more mature and knowledgeable about the evil in which we are willy-nilly implicated—usually in the name of preserving something we feel is right and good, like "our way of life."

The Twilight Zone that began to fall upon North America after the euphoria of the countercultural decade continues to fall; it is the sociohistorical context in which we are now called to think seriously and discover gospel. For me, the postsixties context was the period in which I became (in what I hope is a real and authentic way) a theologian. Everything before 1970—my eleven years of university, seminary, and graduate study; my two years as parish pastor; my three years as college principal; and the first half of my professorship of theology in the Canadian West—I now see as a kind of apprenticeship. During that approximately twenty-year period, I learned some of the necessary skills of my trade and began tentatively to apply them. How fortunate I was to have such master teachers! How fortunate to have such patient and kind parishioners there in little Blind River, good people who wanted so touchingly to help me become the scholar they thought I might become. How fortunate I was to have such devoted students, who in those early years of my teaching listened patiently to my long and labored lectures. It was wonderful—and quite undeserved!

But it was all preparation. I could not become a theologian in earnest until I had allowed myself to be plunged into the growing darkness of my own time and place—my own context. As Tillich would have said, I could not really be trusted with "the theological answer" until I had learned for myself "the human question"—in all of its specificity, its here-and-nowness. Hegel similarly declared that the owl of Minerva, the goddess of wisdom, takes its flight only at evening. In the twilight zone, original thought begins to occur. Luther, too, understood this: "I did not learn my theology all at once," he declared, "but I had to search deeper for it—where my temptations took me!"[22] We need to lose our "answers" if we are going to find an answer that actually engages the real question—which is not just the questions we *ask*, but the question that we *are*, individually and collectively.

I wrote my first serious, full-length theological book in a dim basement room of a student residence in the German city of Münster, Westphalia, in 1972–73. I called the book, borrowing the phrase from Archbishop Cranmer's famous prayer, *Lighten Our Darkness: Towards an Indigenous Theology of the Cross.*[23] It was an elaboration upon a smaller book, a sort of programmatic statement called *Hope against Hope*,[24] which I had given first as lectures for the fiftieth anniversary of the Canadian Student Christian Movement and which was subsequently published by the World Student Christian Federation in Geneva. It pleases me more than it should that *Lighten Our Darkness* was republished in 2001 in an enlarged and revised edition, nearly thirty years after the book first appeared.[25] I am going to say more about this book in the next section, because the "Now" in the section's title, "Where I Am Now," refers to a period in my life that begins with the composition and publication of that book. I will conclude this section by addressing the question, "What was it that pushed me into the twilight zone and thus caused me to become, in a more original way, a Christian theologian?" As I said at the beginning, I am not indulging here in a merely private meditation. I firmly believe that until the churches of North America are led more deeply into the darkness of our epoch, they will continue to exist largely on the surface of life and history. I intend, in other words, to use my own experience to say a little of what I think is involved in entering the "darkness"—the darkness in which the light can find us, for it can only find us there.

Pushed by Fatherhood

The first push came from my children. Among many other things, the phrase *the sixties* conjures up for me the time when all four of our children, three girls and one boy, were born. I was already thirty-three when the first baby appeared, so, unlike fathers who beget children at nineteen (as my father did me), I was filled with wonder at the very existence of such an amazing little being as my Katie. Then, as the others came along, I realized that something unprecedented was happening to me. Before the children, I had been very rooted in the present, with an eye to the past. Suddenly the future began to have an existential grip on me. Not just tomorrow, not just a decade hence, but the *future!*

One day, I remember, a young demographer came into my study at the University in Saskatoon and told me that by the year 2026, the human population curve would start going straight up if we continued reproducing ourselves at the present rate. "Of course," he added in the blasé manner of youthful scientists, "in reality this could never happen. What would happen instead would be war and famine and unbelievable pollution and tension between the races and religions and so on. The earth would become nearly uninhabitable." Our last baby—Lucia, we called her—had just been born. And I found myself reckoning: Lucy would not even be sixty years old in 2026. Would my dear little Lucy have the chance to explore old age? What kind of world would it be for her and her contemporaries? You see, the future was beginning to get faces for me. It was no longer an impersonal and abstract thing, as it had been for the bachelor student of theology I had been, talking learnedly about "eschatology."

So much theology has been done by bachelors—people without the eyes of children looking at them day after day with trust. How seriously have even modern Protestant churches taken children? The young? The future with faces?

Pushed by Wise Counsel

A second push into reality—twilight reality—came from a few wise and insightful individuals, among whom my wife (the real scholar of our duo) would have the first place.[26] My fellow Canadians and good friends George P. Grant and Emil Fackenheim, a Christian and a Jewish philosopher, helped me to become contemporary. George Grant, the wisest commentator on North America known to me, helped me to see the flaws in the modern vision that is the ideological basis of the American Dream and its less glamorous (and perhaps more nuanced) Canadian counterpart.[27] Emil Fackenheim, the recently deceased German Jewish scholar of Hegel and theologian of Judaism, made me reflect more profoundly than I had done before on the meaning, for Christians, of the Holocaust. I saw that Christian triumphalism in the post-Auschwitz world is a sickening thing.[28]

Meanwhile, a great many novelists, dramatists, and filmmakers showed me our world in nonideological terms, causing me to remember Tillich's dictum that Art can depict three states: hope, false hope, and hopelessness (and, he said, art in our time overwhelmingly depicts hopelessness). I learned more from the artists and writers of novels than from the social scientists, whose testimony has always seemed to me too easily tainted by ideological interests.

Pushed by Science

Some of the physical sciences—quite surprisingly, given my limited educational background in the sciences—began to get through to me about this time. If the philosophers and artists helped me to see something of the "insides" of our world—its elusive spirit, its zeitgeist—the scientists helped me to think realistically about the world's "outside." In my final years in the Canadian West, from about 1968 until 1975, the academic community finally became aware of what the whole modern enterprise, with its technological quest for mastery and its aggressive anthropocentrism, was doing to the natural order and hence, of course, to itself. Through the leading scientists in our large university, I began to know (what I certainly did not pick up in my theological education) a little about the interrelatedness of such factors as population, pollution, and the degradation of the environment. I even learned the second law of thermodynamics—which, as Sir Charles Snow observed,[29] humanists and theologians have rarely known, let alone contemplated. I could not have written my three books on the theology of stewardship[30] apart from the incentive I received during those years from the life sciences.

Pushed by Encounter with the Marxist World

I was further plummeted into my world by first encounter with what was then called the Second World. Starting in 1972–73, when we lived in Germany and I was writing *Lighten Our Darkness*, I got to know East Germany, Luther's *Heimat*, then called the German Democratic Republic. For nearly twenty years, I traveled back and forth very often between east and west. As a Canadian, I could go to the GDR more easily than could my West German friends. I went back again and again because—for one thing—I found the church there so very real. It was partly the impact of its reality that inspired me to write another book of that period, *The Reality of the Gospel and the Unreality of the Churches*.[31] In that setting, I also learned the concrete meaning of ideology—not only Marxist-Leninist ideology, which was in its popular form so patently and almost childishly ideological, but also Western capitalist ideology, which is far more subtle and has been, in the long run, far more problematic for the peace of the planet.

I also learned, from East German theologians like Heino Falke, Christoph Magirius, and Ingetraut Ludolphy and the Naumburg theological seminary, where Joseph Hamel taught, how Christians can live in the midst of ideological communities and make a difference. We saw that difference in its most dramatic form in 1989–90, when it was the churches, largely, that prevented the revolt against the Marxist-Leninist regime from turning violent. They could do so precisely because they were not part of the establishment. (Please remember that for later.)

Pushed by My Students

Finally, I was thrust into a new consciousness of my world—my context—by my students. I've drawn attention to some of the problems of the sixties, but one of that period's great pluses was that the traditional distance between professors and students was (or could be) considerably lessened. For ten years in the small seminary in Saskatoon, I spent more time listening to students than I did writing books. I wrote no books at all, in fact, until I was in my mid-forties, and part of the reason for that was that my door was open to my students, perhaps to a fault. A good portion of the research for the books that I did write later, however, came from those often interminable conversations with my students, young and not very young men and (later) women, who in some cases had been more deeply exposed to the world than I had.

One of them in particular comes to mind. He was twenty-nine years of age. He had already completed an MA in history, had taught a little, and was very bright. He was an attractive person both physically and as a personality; he was married to a beautiful young woman; he had everything to live for. Then, one fine day, he was told by his doctor that he had, *perhaps*, one year to live. Leukemia. He had come to the theological seminary to see once more whether anything good could come out of Nazareth. He had grown up in the church, had even for a time been evangelically fervent, had thrown that all over; and now here he was, sitting in my classes every day, his earnest face asking me what I might possibly have to say to the likes of him. I knew that he was shaking his fist at God, but he was so nice that he couldn't do it openly. He was still intimidated by the sort of pietism that thinks you have to be nice to God, even if you are mad as hell at "Him."

I found that year that I again had to think through all the questions: God, the Christ, creation, evil, the church, prayer, suffering, death, resurrection—the lot. I had to hear all that with the ears of that young man dying. In some sense, I had to die myself—die, namely, to my well-fashioned answers, my carefully reasoned lectures.

In this way, I learned what I had known for a long time, what my teachers taught me, what my children taught me, what my mentors Grant and Fackenheim and others taught me, what the novelists and scientists taught me—namely, the meaning of that theological alternative to Christian triumphalism that the genius Martin Luther called *theologia crucis*, theology of the cross.

I am still trying to understand that way. It is still "where I am now." For me, Christian theology is, at base, a theology of the cross. My intention in the second section therefore will be to explain that affirmation, so far as I can.

Where I Am Now

Having disclosed some of the basic ingredients that have gone into the mix of my intellectual/spiritual history, I turn to the still more complex matter of the present. The word *now* is a fascinating one linguistically and biblically. It describes a point in time that, chronologically speaking, has already vanished by the time you say "now."

But Christian faith is called to think in another mode besides the chronological. Chronology—clock time—is terribly important for the tradition of Jerusalem, for unlike the tradition of Athens, the Judeo-Christian faith regards history—which is, of course, based on the linear movement of time—as real and meaningful. What has been *has been*. What will be *will be*. The present is the moving edge of time between past and future.

Alongside this strictly chronological understanding of time, biblical faith places another temporal perspective on historical existence. In recent theology, we have called this the *kairos* dimension. If *chronos* means time understood quantitatively—clock time—*kairos* is time understood qualitatively. There are moments in time that are especially clarifying, illuminating. They are moments when what happens to us also happens, strangely, intimately, *in* us. Past and future somehow converge, or seem to. In this *kairos* moment, the now is a moment filled with meaning, meaning that continues to qualify and change our lives long after the immediate chronological experience has passed. For the people of Israel, that *kairos* moment was in particular the exodus, the liberation from slavery in Egypt. For Christians, the central *kairos* moment is the life, death, and resurrection of the Christ. Thus, Saint Paul, when he uses the little word *now* in Romans 3:21, intends us to hear it in this *kairos* sense: "But now," he writes, after summarizing the dilemmas of both Jewish and Gentile life heretofore, "the righteousness of God has been manifested through faith in Jesus Christ." *Now* a new situation pertains. Time has been invaded by eternity, and faith is able in some dim sense to grasp this and to find, as a result, that time itself (*chronos*) has been, is being, shall be changed.

So where am *I* now? In keeping with this opening discourse on the word *now*, my answer will draw heavily upon the *kairos* quality of time. I would have to say that the now in which I find myself is one that began to disclose itself, chronologically speaking, approximately thirty years ago. In dating this clarifying moment, I certainly would not like to suggest that my mind has been unchanged in thirty years! Charles Hodge, the famous Princeton theologian of another epoch, once boasted that he had not changed his mind in all of his long career.[32] What an appalling confession—and in all probably an exaggeration, uttered for ulterior, *doctrinal* reasons ("See, *true* Christian teaching is always and everywhere the same"). All thinking persons change their minds. Even to think the same thing, you have to think differently, constantly adjusting your thought and your words to ever-changing circumstances, including the assumptions and the language of your time and place.

Yet each of us experiences moments in time (they may quite literally be moments, or they may be years evolving), moments in which we feel we have been visited by some new clarity, some definitive sense of direction. Revelatory moments. *Kairos* moments. I know that, for me, such clarity, meaning, and direction began to assert itself in or about the year 1969, perhaps a little earlier. The now where I am had, so to speak, its genesis then. It is still working itself out. But it will be best if I explain all this simply as it happened.

THE THEOLOGY OF HOPE

In 1967, the year Canada celebrated its hundredth anniversary as a federation, my closest friend, a German pastor and theologian named Friedrich Hufendiek,[33] came to give a series of lectures at the seminary in the western Canadian city of Saskatoon, where I taught for a decade. Fritz and I had been fellow students at Union Seminary, and our friendship now extends to three generations of family and a great network of friends on both sides of the Atlantic.

We were born in the same year, 1928, but given the vastly different contexts in which we lived, our youths were very different. When I was sixteen and just beginning to work in a newspaper office in a prosperous little city in southwestern Ontario, Fritz Hufendiek, having lied about his age so that he could get in on the fight for the Fatherland before it ended—in victory for Germany, as he thought—was sent to the eastern front. What his country got instead of a glorious victory was, of course, an ignoble defeat; and what my friend got was wounded—badly. It was just at the end of the war, and he came home—after a harrowing time in a Russian prison camp (fortunately, he was transferred to the Americans)—a broken spirit and body at age seventeen. This exposure to the darkness of his time led Fritz Hufendiek to the study of Christian theology. He studied under two of the giants of German theology at that time, Helmut Gollwitzer and Hans-Joachim Iwand.

Fritz Hufendiek's story parallels almost exactly the story of another young German, just two years older than Fritz and I: Jürgen Moltmann. Moltmann's new book was to be the topic of Fritz Hufendiek's lectures in Saskatoon in 1967. That book, *The Theology of Hope*, had first appeared in 1965. The English translation of the original German came out in 1967,[34] just as my friend was telling us about it out there in the Canadian West. Nobody in our circle—and only a handful in the English-speaking world generally—had ever heard of the book or of its author.

I listened to these lectures of my friend with growing excitement. Moltmann's analysis of Western civilization as verging on despair struck me as being right on: the "twilight zone" I described in the previous section. I admired immensely the way in which Moltmann interpreted God's transcendence not in spatial but in temporal terms. The transcendent, the divine Source of our hope, is not something that comes to us from *above* (spatial) but from *the future*—God's future (temporal). In Christ, the triune God comes to us with possibilities that do not inhere in our past, in our human performance, in our "works," in our history. The new (*novum*) comes to meet us. "Behold," says the God of Jewish and Christian scripture (e.g., Rev 21:5 NRSV), "I am making all things new." So we must not be fatalized by our past, by the heavy weight of historical cause and effect, by our own blundering attempts at history making. God breaks the vicious circle of historical cause and effect and offers us new beginnings.

You can imagine that in the devastating aftermath of World War II—devastating for Germany especially—this message was received with great enthusiasm by significant numbers of young Germans. Moltmann's book became an almost instant best-seller in his homeland.

Though my own cultural background was quite different (I shall expand on that later in this section), I was able to identify with Moltmann's analysis, partly because some of the primary influences upon Moltmann theologically were also my own—though I found it unfortunate that Moltmann, like most German religious thinkers, had little knowledge of the thought of Reinhold Niebuhr, who could have given his analysis a greater concreteness than it had. But Moltmann came, as I did, out of a new encounter with the Reformation, and through Gollwitzer and Iwand (also *his* teachers), he was deeply influenced by aspects of Karl Barth's thought.

But to this mix, Moltmann added something new (at least it was new to me): the thought of the nondoctrinaire Marxist thinker Ernst Bloch. Bloch, unlike the more ideologically correct Marxists of the time, did not think the redemptive element an inherent principle in the historical process. That is to say, for him, history did not contain its own resolution or salvation. So the new society would not come about automatically or as a matter of time's inevitable progress, as official Marxists thought. Rather, for Bloch the future contained *possibilities*—possibilities inconsistent with the past, discontinuous with history. These possibilities could be grasped by the human intellect and will that had been sufficiently freed from capitalist ideology, modern individualism, and the Western grab for power and gain.[35]

I found Moltmann's interpretation of gospel for today so intriguing that I began to apply it to all kinds of theological and ethical issues—even sex, that little, sad god of our contemporary culture.[36] Certainly it had to be applied also to the growing dilemma of our human relatedness to the rest of creation. We could, if we were liberated from the old, technological image of human mastery, open ourselves to new ways of living in and with nature, not above it, not against it. We did not need to feel trapped in the modern idea of human sovereignty and the technological manipulation of nature. And we certainly did not need to find that notion in the scriptures, which think of the human being not as creation's lord and master, but as nature's conscious child and steward.

Moltmann's eschatological insights—his theology of hope—gave me a new perspective on the relation of faith to the future. The "future shock" that Alvin Toffler and others were detailing was such a shock only because Western peoples had been conditioned to assume that the future would confirm—and confirm ever more conspicuously—our high expectations of its favorable disposition toward our own species, toward our white race, toward our own allegedly advanced Euro-American culture. I felt that Moltmann's work signaled a new kind of lease on life for this old, established religion that had become so very predictable and, to many of our contemporaries, so very boring.

But then, over the next two or three years, I watched with growing dismay what was happening to Moltmann's theology of hope in our North American churches and society. As many of you will know, his book became something of a publishing event when it was translated into English. The religious and secular press got hold of it; newspapers and popular journals made much of it. Pretty soon there were conferences and symposia and seminars everywhere under the theme "Theology of Hope." Every other sermon in the mainstream Protestant churches had to do with hope. Such a lovely, positive word!

I honestly think that very, very few people—including the teaching theologians who talked about the book in their classes—actually read it. All the way through, I mean. I did, and I soon realized that it is, in fact, a very difficult book, requiring a lot of careful attention, rereading, and accompanying research. Nobody in our English-speaking world, for instance, knew anything at all about Ernst Bloch and his kind of Marxism. But one had the feeling that people didn't think they needed to read the book. The slogan was enough! "Theology of hope." Here was another splendid religious motto, made in Germany and therefore undoubtedly deep. We could easily adapt it to our very hope-affirming, nay, our hope-*demanding* North American society. It was a nice way of putting those doom-and-gloom people in their places—those awful "death of God" people, for instance. God was not dead. God was alive and well and sending us positive messages from Tübingen, Germany!

THE THEOLOGY OF HOPE IN AN OFFICIALLY OPTIMISTIC SOCIETY

As I intimated in the first section, I had not published anything much before this time. But now the Holy Spirit (or perhaps it was the unholy one!) got hold of me and insisted that I must certainly do something about this gross misappropriation of Moltmann's theology of hope. I wrote my first serious theological essay then. I called it "The Theology of Hope in the Officially Optimistic Society."[37] What Moltmann was saying in his book, I argued, was addressed to a despairing, defeated, and spiritually empty society: Europe in general, but especially his pathetically reduced Germany, the nation that had thought itself destined for world mastery and now lay in ruins. Moltmann, who had been a prisoner of war in Scotland from 1945 to 1948,[38] had returned from war, as my friend Fritz Hufendiek and thousands of other young Germans had done, devoid of national pride and ready to reconsider the Christian message of radical sin and radical grace. That was the sociohistorical context of the book he wrote.

To take the message of that book out of its context and apply it, with hardly a twist of the theological wrist, to the United States and Canada, winners of the war, was like taking the comfort offered the dying and heaping it holus-bolus on the vigorous, who lived by repressing every thought of death. We U.S. and Canadian North Americans (I exclude Mexico from this generalization, for it tells another story) have been a congenitally—perhaps even a pathologically—optimistic people. Sydney Hook spoke of our "national philosophy of optimism," and church historian Sydney Mead refers to the idea of inevitable progress that gripped the USA in the nineteenth century as "standing on a teleological escalator"[39]—ever upward!

Now, genuine optimism, when it is found (a very rare thing), is lovely to behold. I have a son who is genuinely optimistic, so I know what real optimism looks like. But the optimism of twentieth-century America and beyond is not, I think, very genuine. It is a programmed, promotional, rhetorical optimism—a determined and, increasingly, a desperate determination to think positively, to eliminate the negative, and to have no truck with what Reinhold Niebuhr called "the ambiguities of history." (As George W. Bush so tellingly put it, "I don't do nuance.") Every public figure gives voice to this "official optimism." They must! It is the litany that must accompany the embattled and tarnished American Dream and its aforementioned pale Canadian version. The more that dream has been assailed by time, the more insistently the note of positive thinking has had to be accentuated.

The churches (so I argued in my essay) have on the whole and with few exceptions been more than willing to supply whatever backing they could for this official, ersatz optimism. Whenever the going gets tough and the public cannot dispel its incipient, unacknowledged despair by going shopping or shooting off guns in video arcades or (better still) finding real or imagined enemies to shoot at, there is a certain pressure on the spiritual leaders of our society to bring out their big arguments for hopefulness. But what this public really needs, I argued, is something like a frame of reference for its growing experience of negation; some vantage point from which to take in the negative dimensions of existence without being wholly debilitated by the experience. The data of despair are all around us—in the very air we breathe, in the food we eat, in the god-awful television that we watch, in the poverty, crime, chaos, and violence of our cities. But we have to repress it, as Ernest Becker said in his seminal book *The Denial of Death*,[40] because we have lost touch with any narrative, any perspective that would allow us honestly to contemplate our subconscious, hidden fear and anxiety. We have been so conditioned to believe (as Martin Buber said with ironic intent) that "it will grow ever lighter," that we are wholly disoriented by the deepening darkness.[41] Our foundational religion is not really Christianity but (in George P. Grant's edifying term) "the religion of progress." That religion leaves no peg on which to hang the antithetical experience: that of regress, disappointment, failure. It is said that one Canadian in four today is clinically depressed, but our public rhetoric continues to assure us that we North Americans inhabit the best place in the world in which to live, and the most successful churches back this up with the happy news that we are indeed God's chosen people.

But surely, I said (I am still giving you a digest of that first major essay of mine), surely Christianity has at its very center what is precisely a "frame of reference for the experience of negation." It's called the cross.

Ah! but the truth is that we Christians have subtly rendered *that* perspective ineffectual. Our North American Protestant version of the cross of Christ is not only factually and liturgically empty, it is empty symbolically as well. We've made it nothing more than a prelude to the great Victory of the Third Day. For popular Christianity (whose popularity has precisely to do with this fact), the resurrection renders the cross of Jesus a thing of the past. We live on this side of Easter! The whole story of Jesus' passion, death, and resurrection seems to most people in our society something like a stained-glass version of the Horatio Alger paradigm. The cross is the necessary poor-boy prelude to the great success called Easter. You can't keep a good man down! Thus, the cross as such tends to be unconnected with the real pain and alienation that people experience. It signifies what has been overcome, defeated, surpassed. It speaks of a reality that is no more. For true-believing faith, there is no more death, no more suffering, no more sorrowing, no more despair, no more evil. Though we live in the midst of life's negations, we live as those who know that they have already been refuted by a victorious Savior—at least for the redeemed. Many, especially in the United States, regarding their *nation* as essentially Christian, could apply such theo-logic to America as a whole and so conclude that if there are great evils in the world, their causes must be sought for beyond these Christian borders.

CROSS AND CONTEXT

In short, in this early essay I began to explore two of the themes that became—and have continued to be—my chief vocational mandate:

(1) contextuality (you can't take a gospel for defeated Germany and offer it straightaway as a gospel for victorious America); and (2) the theology of the cross. But from the first, I meant the theology of the cross not as a theoretical or merely historical phenomenon—and certainly not as an exercise in Luther research—but as address, as engagement of our actual situation as a people. I meant the theology of the cross understood as gospel—gospel for a desperately optimistic people, a fearful and covertly despairing people afraid of expressing its fearfulness and lostness. "The only thing we have to fear," said Franklin D. Roosevelt in 1933, "is fear itself." He must have sensed, already then, the propensity of this "New World" society of ours (our rhetorical optimism notwithstanding) to become so fearful about our condition that we would be willing to sacrifice all the "values" that had made us new in order to have security.

This was the frame of mind in which, at age forty-four, I finally qualified for my first sabbatical leave. With Rhoda and our four little children, I went off to Germany in 1972 to write a book, following fairly closely the smaller book, *Hope against Hope*, that had resulted from my lectures for the fiftieth anniversary of the Canadian Student Christian Movement and was subsequently published by the World Student Christian Federation. I went to Germany, partly because my friend Fritz could put up our entire family of six in his big apartment on the campus of the university in Münster, partly because I needed to come to terms with the German experience, out of which so much Christian theology has arisen, and partly because, in order to understand one's own culture, one has to get some distance away from it.

In the meantime, someone[42] had seen to it that Moltmann got a copy of my programmatic essay about the theology of hope in our officially optimistic society, and I received a very encouraging note from Moltmann himself. So, shortly after our arrival in Münsterland, I took up Moltmann's invitation and went to see him in Tübingen.

I was surprised—and extremely gratified—to learn then about his present work. He was hard at work on his next book after *The Theology of Hope*, a book that he would call *Der gekreuzigte Gott* (*The Crucified God*),[43] one of the most shocking terms of Martin Luther. It was shocking because in the Middle Ages (and not only then), you didn't speak about *God* as suffering, but only the Christ. God was above all that!

Because my own thinking had been moving in the same direction, I asked Moltmann why—for goodness' sake!—he had taken on such a theme as this, after the great success of his theology of hope. He replied that in the light of the actual reception of his *Theology of Hope*, he found it necessary to explain that *Christian* hope was not to be confused with Western civilization's Enlightenment optimism, but was based on the cross of Christ. He felt that he had to counter the misuse of his first book by saying now, in this second one, that the theology of hope is a chapter in the theology of the cross. His *Theology of Hope*, he said, had been almost as badly understood in Germany as it was in North America. Between his initial formulation of the thought presented in *The Theology of Hope* and its actual publication, something had occurred that he had not sufficiently taken into account, namely, the German economic miracle, the so-called German Phoenix, that had turned his countrymen away from the sober contemplation of their devastating, foolish, and pretentious past toward yet another kind of secular messianism. They stand on the bridges over the autobahn, he said, and watch with pride and adulation the swift parade of Mercedes and other fast cars. They are not in the mood for honesty about their recent history. Too many of them, if they were familiar with his theology of hope, had turned it into cheap hope, a version of Bonhoeffer's "cheap grace."[44] The future was going to be great; Germany would be the winner after all! What he had to do now, Moltmann said, was to demonstrate, for those who had ears to hear, that the only way Christians can dare to speak about hope is by standing not on bridges over the autobahn, but beneath the cross, waiting in the darkness of Golgotha for the light that shines in the darkness. Otherwise, gospel becomes nothing more than a stained-glass adaptation of the trendy technocratic utopianism of the consumer society—bourgeois transcendence with a thin patina of sentimental theism.

When I returned to Münster to write the book that became *Lighten Our Darkness: Towards an Indigenous Theology of the Cross*, I felt that I was trying to do for my own context exactly what the modest and thoughtful Moltmann was doing for his. In another part of that same Teutonic forest, Dorothee Soelle was also thinking along these lines. And in Asia so were Kazoh Kitamori, Kosuke Koyama, Shusaku Endo, and C. S. Song. A new critical, constructive, and socially conscious theology of the cross was being born. Since then, it has achieved an impressive flowering, though it remains and is no doubt destined to remain a minority tradition.

THE *CANTUS FIRMUS*

Where am I *now*? The theology of the cross remains for me, since it began to be definitively thirty years ago, the *cantus firmus*, the dominant motif of all my thought and writing. It is the *kairotic* now in which I remain poised and expectant, hoping to understand it more and more fully, trying to comprehend its relevance to the problems and possibilities that are quite literally new every morning. In the next section, I shall directly address some of these new or more fully emerging realities. The theology of the cross is my *foundational* theology.

Yet I confess that I am somewhat uncomfortable about the terminology. In the first place, the theology of the cross is not an *it*; it is not yet another "theology of"; it is not a doctrine or a system of doctrines; it is not even a school. It is a spirit and a method, a way of seeing the world, a mode of reflecting on historical experience and on the tradition that has been handed over to us. As Moltmann put it in an excellent metaphor, the theology of the cross is not a particular chapter in Christian theology, it is the "key signature" in which Judeo-Christian theology is and must be played.[45] It affects every dimension, every area of doctrine, every ethical question, every liturgical expression. It has as much to do with our anthropology as with our doctrine of God, our doctrine of the church as our doctrine of the Christ, our understanding of our mission as our conception of the Christian life.

In the last two decades of the twentieth century, my decision to attempt an extensive, systematic study of Christian theology in our North American context was based on this pre-understanding:[46] If the theology of the cross is indeed the key signature of all Christian theology, then one should try to apply this spirit and this method to all the aspects of Christian faith. Moreover, because the theology of the cross is above all a concrete and (in Bonhoeffer's sense) a "this-worldly" theology, it would be necessary at every point to work out such a systematic articulation of this theology in relation to the specific realities of one's own time and place, one's own context. It would be no theology of the cross that took the results of another people's struggle with its history (the Germans', for example) and simply reproduced its lessons in one's own quite different context. A genuine theology of the cross would have to mean entering as deeply as possible into the actual experiences of one's own people and, out of that explicit history and culture with its particular problems and impasses, trying to find some way into the future.

In that frame of mind, I undertook the work that resulted in three big volumes: *Thinking the Faith*, *Professing the Faith*, and *Confessing the Faith*, each with the subtitle *Christian Theology in a North American Context*.[47] In my most recent book, *The Cross in Our Context: Jesus and the Suffering World*,[48] I have continued, updated, and consolidated that same attempt at understanding Christian faith for our time and place.

Since more formal and technical expressions of my understanding of the *theologia crucis* can be found in those and other published works, I prefer now to speak of this tradition in a rather different way. It will require examining broadly cultural as well as personal aspects of the background that I have brought to this theological tradition. Traditions only become for us what they can become when they enter into conversation with our own souls, even at the risk of undergoing a certain alteration. Otherwise (to evoke Jaroslav Pelikan's nice distinction between tradition and traditionalism),[49] they remain at the level of "dead faith."

THE SPIRIT OF THIS THEOLOGY

I've said that the theology of the cross describes a spirit and method of theological reflection; it does not restrict itself to any one doctrinal area but colors the whole account of reality that we call Christian. How should one describe this spirit and method? I will try to do so here in two stages, beginning with a broad historical generalization.[50] It is a generalization about the cultural context in which the theology of the cross was first named and has in various ways and degrees been kept alive: the Germanic. I will contrast that context with Anglo-Saxon culture, especially in the latter's modern expression. Like all such generalizations, this one will leave many questions unanswered and perhaps invite the charge of oversimplification. Nevertheless, it expresses an important dimension of what I have found over the course of several decades to be necessary background for acquiring an adequate appreciation for this theological approach. To describe my own theological journey, I must therefore risk such a generalization.

The second stage in my attempt to characterize the spirit of the *theologia crucis* will be more immediately personal, and I would hesitate to indulge in such autobiographical reflection in any public medium other than one intended to reveal something of one's own spiritual history. Here I will address briefly the question, What can I detect in my personal experience and (so far as I can even understand it) my character that might have drawn me to this "not much loved" (Moltmann) theological tradition? The connecting thread between these two small investigations could be expressed in this way: Though I am quite clearly a member of the Anglo-Saxon tribe and in every part of my being influenced by the great aims, ambitions, and assumptions of that tribe (its practicality, activism, devotion to common sense, even its optimism), I have never been wholly convinced of the generally positive outlook that prevails among the English-speaking peoples in their various forms and permutations, however much I may admire their political and other achievements. Life is simply more difficult than it is made out to be in most of the stories they tell. There are heights and also depths that those stories do not comprehend. The more I have witnessed the kinds of human and global dilemmas that are created by our "innocent," activist, and well-meaning Anglo-American superpower, the more I am drawn to the premodern, preindustrial worldviews that retain, in spite of

everything, some memory of older tales about the human journey—
and my own.

GERMANIC BACKGROUND OF THIS THEOLOGY

Beginning with the historical generalization, my experience has been
that the theology of the cross is so foreign to the social and religious
ethos of our prevailing culture that—even in many Lutheran circles in
North America—it is necessary to engage in a good deal of discussion
before something approaching understanding may occur. The Anglo-
Saxon world to which I belong has operated under the influence of assumptions and values that, if not inimical to this faith posture, make it
difficult to grasp either intuitively or analytically. With few exceptions,
our approach to the world has been linear, not dialectical; straight-
forward, not paradoxical; and pragmatic, not mystical. In contrast,
dialectic, paradox, and mystery are all at the heart of this theological
approach. In the traditions of English-speaking empiricism, we tend
to mistrust any thinking that is not grounded in sensory experience
and/or verifiable data. I once heard a young philosopher trained in
the empiricist-linguistic tradition dismiss Søren Kierkegaard, Martin
Heidegger, Jean-Paul Sartre, and all existentialism as "poetry." On the
one hand, we may nod in good-humored agreement with the proverb
that "things are seldom what they seem," but when it comes to daily
life, we want to stick to the facts and avoid what is likely to seem to us
speculation, if not sheer fantasy.

The dominant Germanic traditions of philosophy, theology, literature, and the arts are, in this respect at least, quite different. The
difference is more transparent in the arts than in most other areas.
To say it briefly, Brahms's *Requiem* could not have been composed
by an Englishman, nor Thomas Mann's *Doctor Faustus* written by an
American, Australian, or Canadian. To some extent, similar observations may be made about French, Italian, Spanish, and other European approaches to reality, but because we are concerned here about
a tradition shaped by (and shaping) the Protestant experience, it is
expedient to concentrate on the Germanic side of this distinction. In
a way that is not true of mainstream Anglo-Saxon culture, the Ger-

manic peoples retained aspects of the premodern world, including the old pagan as well as the medieval worldviews. In the Germanic lands, those earlier conceptions of reality did not give way as easily as they did in the English-speaking world to modernity's essential one-dimensionality and anthropocentrism. While the modern vision accentuated the power of free, rational, history-making Homo sapiens over the raw forces of nature and the irrational dimensions of human nature, the older worldviews maintained a profound and fearsome respect for destiny (fate, in pagan terms), the irrational and chaotic, and the perennially tragic element in all of humankind's efforts and enterprises.

Now, none of the key words that I have used in the previous sentence can find a familiar home in minds that have been fashioned by modern Anglo-Saxon experience and rhetoric: To propose that we are creatures of *destiny* is to run headlong into the most sacred concept of the English-speaking world, especially of the United States of America: freedom. To object to some project of the technological society on the basis of its failure to respect the *irrational* and *chaotic* in nature and human nature (that is, on the basis of its assumption that natural chaos can be controlled and chance eliminated) is to invite the scorn not only of the technocrats but of most ordinary citizens, schooled in the can-do conventions of human mastery over nature. And if the word *tragic* is used in some such way as to suggest application to the human condition generally, not just an untimely death or unfortunate public occurrence, the mind shaped by basic modern assumptions will feel intuitively that it is in the presence of something strange and dark indeed.[51]

Certainly, Christianity, too, challenges all those words—these great negations—and the ominous realities they name. But the kind of Christianity that emerges will depend upon how the word *challenges* in that sentence is interpreted. Whether in its Calvinist, Methodist-pietist, or Anglican forms, the tendency in Anglo-Saxon Protestantism, especially but not exclusively in its modern expressions, has been to regard this challenge as a synonym for *overcome*: Christian freedom *overcomes* whatever limitations inhere in our "destiny"; the ordering of life by the sovereign Lord of the gospel *overcomes* the irrationality and chaos of existence; the victory of the Christ over death and evil *overcomes* the tragic element in individual and corporate human life. In short, the negative component in every case is negated by a triumphant positive. The "already" dimension of Christian eschatology is dominant.

But challenge can be understood in another way, namely, as an ongoing struggle, a stubborn refusal to submit to what presents itself as inevitability, and an abiding sense that the power of that which negates, even in moments when its power seems invincible, is *nevertheless* (appearances to the contrary) being countered by something that is life-affirming and "on our side," as in a famous line from Luther's hymn, "Were not the right man on our side, our striving would be losing."[52] In this view, the great antitheses—destiny, chaos, the tragic (and, of course, these do not exhaust the list)—are challenged, certainly, but not overcome, not already relegated to the old dispensation. An eschatological *not yet* is here in dialectical tension with the *already* that faith glimpses "through a glass darkly."

Such a conception of the Christian challenge cannot present the Christian gospel as an already-complete setting aside of the old in favor of the new. It cannot speak of faith as though disbelief and doubt were empty spiritual categories. It cannot advance a vision of hope that has no more traffic with despair. It cannot affirm life as though death and its "sting" (Paul) were passé, or of love as though it could ever be (in us!) unmixed with ulterior motives, or of the good as though all evil had already been put to flight, or of knowledge as though ignorance and the human resistance to truth had been mastered. The theology that emerges from such a pre-understanding of the "challenge" of the Christian message will therefore necessarily be a theology that deals in struggle, the clash of opposites (polarities),[53] paradox, and mystery. It will not be a finished product but a commentary on what is still going on. It will not provide a resolution of all life's contradictions but only a framework of courage on whose basis one may participate more fully in real life without being crushed by the negations that are part of life (see 2 Cor 4:8-13).

The theology of the cross is such a theology.

Luther, the German, the still-medieval man, the peasant become scholar, the mystic activist—this Luther whose peculiar sensitivity enabled him to name this biblical tradition so imaginatively, in all his key concepts tries to do justice to the dialectical interplay of old and new, darkness and light, negative and positive to which the Christian vocation invites one. God is both revealed and concealed—concealed in his revelation, revealed in his concealment. The triumph of grace in the cross of Christ is hidden from the eyes of flesh—hidden, indeed, beneath its apparent opposite. The glory and power of God are made manifest in weakness and suffering, the weakness of the child of Bethlehem, the suffering of the crucified one. The good news that calls the church into being is absurdity to the learned and offense to the religious. Human "good works" are never *really* good, since even the noblest of them are the products of very questionable, usually prideful motivation, so they do not "justify." They do not lend us credence and authenticity; only trust in Another does that, and that trust (faith) is neither "sight" nor free of its antithesis, mistrust and doubt. Thus, the Christian is *simul justus et peccator*—not one or the other, and not just a little of each, part justified, part sinner, but wholly and simultaneously both. There can be greater, more authentic piety in a man's curses than in the sanctimonious prayers of the religious. As for radical evil, the devil (for Luther a grim reality) is by no means inactive after his effective (proleptic) defeat by the incarnate Word. The great deceiver is nowhere more subtly at work than wherever true faith is found. In fact, one of the surest marks of authentic faith is its periodic sense of total abandonment—the *Anfechtungen*, to use Luther's own term.[54]

Now, to those whose cultural predisposition inclines them toward the first conception of what the Christian "challenge" would have to mean, the theology of the cross will seem inconclusive. Or worse! It may well appear pre-Christian,[55] crypto-pagan, or even atheistic. The term *dualism* will sometimes be used about it, for God and Satan, good and evil, light and darkness seem still to contend here in a manner abhorrent to all who embrace the unconditional sovereignty of God. Reading Luther, the average Canadian Anglican or American Presbyterian or Methodist will feel that he or she is being assailed by contradictory claims. Indeed, Luther's very life can seem a life chock-full of contradiction, as Martin E. Marty has persuasively argued in his recent Penguin biography of the Reformer.[56] One does not have to approve all the contradictions in Luther's person, however, to recognize that many of his ideas are not contradictions at all, but paradoxes. Moreover, they are such, not on account of a perverse Germanic preference for intellectual gymnastics or obscurantism, but because for Luther life itself is a battleground of opposing forces—a belief in which Luther mirrors, as he does so frequently, the Pauline tradition:

> So I find it to be a law that when I want to do what is good, evil lies close at hand. For I delight in the law of God in my inmost self, but I see in my members another law at war with the law of my mind, making me a captive to the law of sin that dwells in my members. Wretched man that I am! Who will rescue me from this body of death? Thanks be to God through Jesus Christ our Lord! (Rom 7:21-25 NRSV)

In a way that is almost unique in Christian history, though it has echoes of Augustine's *Confessions*, Luther constantly gives voice to his own moral foibles and intellectual limitations. To be sure, he did not express this in the hand-wringing way of that Melanchthon to whom, in frustration, he cried, "Sin boldly!" but with extraordinary frankness: "We are beggars—that's for sure!"[57] This exceptionally honest late-medieval soul simply could not indulge in premature and exaggeratedly positive religious claims at the expense of life. Precisely that was what he despised about the theology that he contrasted with his *theologia crucis*—what he called *theologia gloriae*, the theology of glory (in our terms, religious triumphalism). In the name of religious certitude and finality, it had to end by lying about reality—by turning faith into sight, hope into consummation, the resurrection into proof of the Christ's divinity and visible victory, the church into the kingdom of God, and so forth. In short, the *theologia gloriae* offers people a perfected and already-redeemed state—so long as they can keep their eyes shut.[58]

To all whose spirituality has been shaped by the typical assumptions of our Anglo-Saxon culture and cultus, especially in its modern versions, such a faith is likely to seem unsatisfactory—simply not enough. As can be seen plainly in many expressions of Christianity in the English-speaking world today and in new Asian and African churches deeply influenced by missionary activity emanating from that world, what our culture demands of religion is that it should provide the resolution of the whole human predicament—if not fully and visibly, with at least sufficient weight to tip the balances unmistakably in that direction: if not in this world here and now, then by all means in "the next." We are not satisfied with the *confidence* (*con + fide*) that faith offers; we want certitude. If the majority of people in our society are going to opt into any faith, any worldview, religious or secular, they want something that answers every great question or at least provides a spiritual atmosphere in which decisive answers can seem immanent, viable, demonstrable. Given the sociological mythology of attainability (instant everything!) by which our society is driven at every level, it is hard to live in the midst of irresolution, prolonged tension, conspicuous incompleteness. The feelings and rhetoric that preceded the most recent war in Iraq fairly hummed with the sentiment "Why equivocate? Let's do it! Let's get it over with!" (And how pathetically the aftermath of that war has demonstrated the folly of such an "over with.") People want what has become a favorite word in public discourse of late: closure. And if they still look to religion, it is to provide the *kind* of closure that cannot be provided by politics, war, technology, the acquisition of things, or the medical, psychiatric, and chemical wonders of late modernity.

But the point is that precisely such "closure" cannot be given. The whole notion of finality, where creatures of time are concerned, is entirely understandable as desire but impossible, inherently deceptive, and always potentially dangerous. Dangerous, because those who are ideologically committed to some version of historical finality will always, if they have the external power to do so, strive to make the world conform to their preconception of it. The Nazis did that. Marxism-Leninism did that. The political and religious Right in the United States of America today is trying to do just that.

Even in the microcosmic world of personal life and relationships, the quest for wholly satisfactory endings is at least elusive when it is not downright fictitious. A rebellious son, resentful of his father's authority, wants the death of his father to bring closure to his lifelong struggle with his father. Well, it is true that the father, being dead, will no longer play an active role in the troubled relationship, but does the son imagine that the father's physical absence will end his struggle with his father? To the contrary: now wholly internalized, that struggle could well become yet more intense and preoccupying. The parents of a murdered daughter await with eagerness the closure that the murderer's execution will bring them (or so they tell the media). Perhaps if they are very naive, they will for a time even mistake this act of publicly sanctioned revenge for some kind of release from their grief over the loss of their child. But what does this second death resolve? For the thoughtful, nothing at all. It only adds to a cruel incompleteness a further burden of emptiness.

But when people turn to religion for its capacity to resolve not only a crime or a bad relationship or a death, but also evil, alienation, and mortality as such, they are seeking a great deception. A religion that essays to supply that demand—whether in immediate this-worldly or consoling otherworldly terms—is catering to the very temptations that the Christ withstood in the wilderness. Not only is it guilty of capitalizing on the most cowardly instinct of finite creatures, namely, the instinct to flee the creaturely state, but it is at the same time allowing its message and its "sanctuary" to become a place of escape and the massive repression of reality.

Western civilization, particularly in its Anglo-Saxon expressions, can—at its high points and in comparison with other civilizations—be interpreted as a kind of human success story. Undoubtedly, this is due in no small measure precisely to the very positive outlook that has driven it in its modern forms. A society in its ascendancy, like a young adult at the zenith of his or her physical and mental powers, can only be spurred to greater achievements by a cultural mythos that accentuates the possibilities for continuous growth and the pushing aside of all barriers. "New World" ideology and rhetoric are famous for their exploitation of just this mythos. And the secular dimension of the myth has been undergirded from the outset by the religious dimension: the Christianity that was able to transform challenges to humanity into victories all but won already.

But Western civilization is no longer in its ascendancy. It is opposed now by civilizations it has been taught to regard as inferior and by critical and vocal elements within its own precincts. It is opposed even more by its increasingly visible failure to deliver the utopias promised by its rhetoric. Its well-rehearsed stories of success ring hollow now. The extravagant claims of the American Dream have been replaced by the essentially negative aims of America's present-day leadership, which promises, not to "put a chicken in every pot," but to protect a frightened public against the threats, real and imagined, of terrorists. It is said that September 11, 2001, "changed everything." That, too, is an exaggeration. The terrorist attacks of that horrific moment did not *effect* the change; they only announced—for those who had not noticed it earlier—a change that had been transpiring for decades: a change in the mythos that had been the spiritual underpinning of modernity.

Reinhold Niebuhr, almost uniquely among white American Christian thinkers, had discerned that change more than half a century earlier. His face—a worried, skeptical, but touchingly compassionate face—appeared on the cover of the twenty-fifth anniversary issue of *Time* in 1948. In the background are dark and tumultuous clouds, and on the horizon, a cross. The heading below the picture reads, "Man's Story Is Not a Success Story."[59]

The question confronting serious Christians in the West today is whether the Christian faith is able to address a civilization no longer on the rise but falling, visibly in decline—and tempted in its decline, as ancient Rome was, to seek its continued glory and power in ever more aggressive and bellicose acts, designed by leaders who do not "do nuance." We can see before us, plainly displayed, how the old, typically English-speaking Christianity of our past functions in this internally changed society. Its triumphalism, whether in fundamentalist otherworldly or liberal this-worldly guise, contributes to the most imperialistic of the political alternatives available to us. This should not surprise us; the theology of glory has always intuitively sought and found its counterpart in a politics of glory.

Only a theology that is capable of realism—capable, in Luther's words, of "calling the thing what it really is"[60]—can prove appropriate and prophetic in a society where "success stories" are credible only to the naive or the willfully uninformed, and where "challenges" do not automatically give way to victories but must be lived with. The cross that is at the center of the Christian confession of faith in God has long been co-opted, in our Anglo-Saxon milieu, by our cultural triumphalism, which, by exploiting (and distorting) the resurrection, has effectively emptied the cross of its significance as a point of reference for human suffering and hope. The question facing us (if I may now refine its earlier statement) could be, Can we Christians now, in these once-overconfident Anglo-Saxon societies of the West, present a Christian gospel in which the resurrection of Jesus Christ is able still to speak to the human hope for "a happy issue out of all our troubles," but *without minimizing* the "troubles" and thus making this faith available only to those who are adept at repression? Can we offer our contemporaries a gospel that helps them courageously affirm their creaturehood while keeping their eyes wide open?

The best help we can find, if such a project grasps us, is in the various past and present expressions of the theology of the cross. Yet most of them (not all, but most) lie outside the experience and the literature of our dominant Anglo-Saxon religious and cultural conventions. There can be no question of simply importing theologies that are "made in Germany" into our significantly different English-speaking contexts. That would be to defeat not only the contextual component of the theological task, but also to misappropriate the theology of the cross itself. For where it is truly understood, this theology drives insistently toward concretization and engagement with the specific world in which it is undertaken. In fact, the entire enterprise of enucleating a culturally specific expression of the *theologia crucis* would be grievously misconceived if it were reduced to an attempt to imitate or implant this or that German, Scandinavian, or other version of this theology, as sometimes happens in self-consciously Lutheran circles. For one thing, North American religious history demonstrates that such attempts do not enter the mainstream of the culture but are confined to ethnic and other minorities. Moreover, the Germanic appropriations of this theological tradition have themselves frequently contained flaws with which the most vigilant exponents of the theology of the cross in recent European history have had to battle. One thinks of Bonhoeffer's fight against the reduction of the "justification" theology of Luther to "cheap grace," or of Moltmann's and Soelle's and others' attempts to overcome the failure of so much conventional Lutheranism to develop a critical *social* ethic. If the theology of the cross is to become a meaningful witness for Christians in Anglo-Saxon societies, it must go well beyond imbibing the results of the spiritual struggles of Protestants in Germanic cultures.

Yet by its nature Christian theology requires dialogue with and help from a "usable past." Theology, unlike popular philosophies, cannot be spun out of one's own or one's culture's immediate experience. It requires a tradition, a past, with which to struggle and from which to learn. And it is beyond question that the "past" of this particular mode of theological reflection in the Protestant mode is to be located principally in the history and literature of Germanic Protestantism. For reasons that are complex and hard to trace, it is out of the cauldron of European and especially German history that the most compelling statements of this theology have emerged. If we who belong to the Anglo-Saxon world today and for decades past have sensed in that literature themes and emphases that we knew we could not ignore, the reason is largely that the religious and theological conventions prevalent in our own seemingly less problematic cultures began to appear too superficial to address the new and profound problems that had found their way, at last, into our midst as well.

The theology of the cross does not arise spontaneously out of the historical experience of a people, but historical experience, including the informing story or mythos of a people, can be a crucible in which this approach to Christian faith and life more readily takes shape. The conflict and chaos of Germanic history, which have given rise to terrible events affecting the entire world, have also constituted a cultural milieu in which aspects of the Hebraic-Christian faith could be grasped and articulated in a manner not common to Christians in more placid social settings. English-speaking Christianity has reflected the relative placidity and self-confidence of Anglo-Saxon societies. Our condition as "winner" societies has in some real sense made it natural for us to appropriate, out of the rich heritage of biblical faith, aspects that accentuate the positive and minimize, if they do not eliminate, the negative and the ambiguous. This has not *always* led to a shallow faith in which "all things bright and beautiful" camouflaged the shadow side of reality, but it has encouraged us, all the same, to hear the Christian message in the biblical tradition that stresses the "already" of God's triumph over all that negates, and remains rather oblivious to the "not yet."

Conversely, the disruptive and in some sense tragic history of the Germanic peoples made for a cultural context in which it was impossible to ignore the unrealized dimension of biblical eschatology. Reinhold Niebuhr noted in *The Nature and Destiny of Man* that Luther had "an inordinate fear of chaos," but Luther came by that phobia honestly enough, for he lived in a chaotic context. Christianity could make sense to him only if it provided a vantage point from which to acknowledge that chaos and confront it with something like courage. He found such a faith in the mingled praise and lament of the psalmists and prophets[61] and in the Pauline testimony to the divine creation *out of nothing*, justification *of sinners*, and resurrection *of the dead*.

But we should make no mistake about it: what Luther found was a *biblical* theology, not just a German theology. The tumultuous cultural background of Luther's life was certainly the occasion—perhaps even the *conditio sine qua non*—of his "discovery" of the theology of the cross, but it was not the substance of that theology. The substance of it is located in the prophetic sense of the "divine compassion" (Abraham Heschel) for our nearly impossible species and the evangelists' proclamation of the victory of the Crucified One—the victory "hidden beneath its opposite."

It may be that *that* victory can be profoundly grasped only by Christian communities whose social contexts manifest conspicuous evidence of the "opposite" beneath which it is hidden. Insofar as that is so, our own emerging cultural context in the Anglo-Saxon lands—our characteristic bravado notwithstanding—may prove a better soil for the growth of the fragile plant called *theologia crucis* than was our placid and optimistic past.

PERSONAL DIMENSION

From the macrocosm, I turn to the microcosm—the self that has been nurtured by, yet never quite belonged to, that so-called Anglo-Saxon world. This second stage in my attempt to characterize the spirit of the *theologia crucis* would, if I were to execute it with anything like completeness, require so much space that I shall not even try for anything like fullness here. In the absence of an extensive autobiography, it will have to suffice to indicate in very terse terms some of the reasons why I have never felt quite at home in my own Anglo-Saxon milieu and why, with some misgivings (because Germanic Protestantism certainly comes replete with its own grievous problems), I have been drawn time after time to people like Nicholas of Cusa, Luther, Kierkegaard, Bonhoeffer, Tillich, Soelle, and other exponents of the faith who rely heavily upon this theological alternative. I will mention four aspects of my experience that contribute to this attraction.

To begin with, I am a Canadian. Although it certainly may not be said of every Canadian, it is decidedly part of our national character that we have an innate awareness of the real difficulty of the human enterprise and an innate skepticism concerning schemes and dreams that minimize that difficulty. This awareness and skepticism has at least two overwhelming causes. One is historical: we never quite lost touch with the older stories of our two founding European cultures, for we never broke with either Britain or France in the dramatic way of our southern neighbor. Those older stories (let us not forget the Celtic!) contained elements inimical to modernity. The second cause, however, is the more important: we inhabit a vast geographic area (second in size only to the former USSR) with a population comparable today to California's, strung out along the Canadian/U.S. border and conscious of the unending and mostly unpeopled miles to the north.

Even though the majority of us now live in cities, "nature" is very, very real in Canada—and on the whole it is inhospitable: beautiful often, but rarely bountiful in the usual sense. The overweening theme of our imaginative literature, both French and English (as Margaret Atwood and others have often shown), is survival, not success. If the Canadian version of the American Dream is a pale one (something of an understatement), it has a good deal to do with the reality checks that nature has introduced into Canadian life. Historically speaking, we have never been able to entertain the ambitions of a major world power; to the contrary, our unenviable destiny is to live on the edge of empire—first the British, then the American. Environmentally, we confront every day the limitations and the indifference to human design that the great forces of nature place upon all human striving. A religion that did not take that into account would automatically limit itself to economically well-insulated city dwellers. A salient factor in the notorious and unapologetic secularity that has come to be in Canada since the end of World War II, I suspect, is conventional Christianity's apparent inability to develop a credible theology of nature. U.S.-based evangelicalism and fundamentalism now look upon a conspicuously dechurched Canada and Quebec as happy hunting grounds, but with the exception of pockets here and there, they will not alter the skeptical northern spirit of this country. I, for one, am grateful for that.

Another important influence is that I am a child of the working classes and of the Great Depression. The general if relative affluence of North America for the past half century has had the unfortunate effect of creating, among those who benefited from it, the illusion of a nearly permanent state of well-being. Most of those now responsible for passing on the wisdom of our culture—the teachers and educators, the journalists and pop sociologists, the media personalities, and others—have had no personal experience of either economic depression or world war. Many of them, even those with a little historical information, are likely to operate out of economic norms and expectations that are of very recent vintage. In Canada, for instance, the media constantly refer to our "traditional" program of universal Medicare—which, after a mere thirty-seven years, can hardly qualify as a tradition.

Those of us who grew up during the "dirty thirties" and "the War" have another, less sanguine pre-understanding of what is normal in human affairs, especially if we are the products of working-class homes. I can remember very well when my father worked six days a week, ten hours a day, with no annual holidays and only four statutory days off during the year. He was glad to have the work for much of the time, as a laid-off or "bumped" railway employee, he was without any gainful employment. With such a formative experience of life in my youth and adolescence, I have always found it hard to believe the great promises of the ideologues of the Right *or* the Left, whether secular or religious.

The third element of this personal dimension is that I was blessed (or burdened?) from my birth with a particular sensitivity concerning the hardships faced by ordinary people. Though I did not myself suffer conspicuously (to the contrary), I seem always to have had what some would consider an inordinate awareness of human suffering. Many people manifest such awareness, and I do not regard it as an achievement or a virtue; it is simply a reality with which, from my earliest childhood consciousness, I have had to cope. When my playmates were able to laugh at old ladies trying to maneuver a busy street, a mentally deficient man attempting to articulate a simple wish, a shy kid from the country, or a "sissy," I could never laugh with them. I felt a kind of personal grief when I heard lonely souls grieving at the funerals of lost parents or lost children, and I often wandered among the tombstones of our village cemetery, thinking about the people memorialized there, especially the young ones.

Was it morbidity? Maybe. But it had another side, too. I wouldn't have felt empathy for the victims of sickness and death and sorrow and all the rest had I not felt just as strongly life's beauty, promise, and potential for joy. "The grandeur and the misery" (Pascal) go together. Those who are unmoved by the joy of life seldom are moved by the pain of life either. The pain was visible at every level in the small village in which I grew up: the old and the ill were fully present among us, the dying usually died at home, family quarrels were everybody's knowledge, and bright children made dull children seem even duller. So long as the pain was there, accounts of the world that failed to recognize it could not speak to me. I knew intuitively and by experience what Thoreau meant when he wrote, "Most [people] live lives of quiet desperation." So the happy-happy people in the advertisements and the Sunday school papers always seemed to me unreal and false.

Finally, in addition to such unsought consciousness of human vulnerability (but not, I suspect, unrelated to it), I am one of those born with an exceptional ear for music. Neither of my parents was musical; my father was tone-deaf, in fact, so I know perfectly well that it is sheer gift. Like the former gift, a deep-seated gift of music is never unambiguously beneficent. For one thing, in a society that worships sports and prefers the extrovert, the child gifted with music is liable frequently to find himself on the sidelines, particularly if he is a boy. At a deeper level, those who are born with unusual sensitivity to sound and whose natural endowment is trained by exposure to great music to experience the depths and heights of human emotion that music (and perhaps music alone) can express—such persons are seldom able to embrace creeds that ignore or minimize the shadow side of human experience. With its strange interplay of minor and major progressions and harmonies, its never wholly predictable turns of phrase and melody, its interacting but sometimes incompatible rhythms, great music mirrors life's many-sidedness and its strange combination of order and capriciousness.

Above all, those who truly *hear* great music cannot escape its tendency to move the spirit in ways that are sometimes almost too much, too poignant. "Every time I listen to classical music," said a young girl in my circle of adolescents, "I end up crying." I understood very well what she meant, and her remark struck me all the more because she was neither a musician herself nor a devotee of music. How could anyone listen to Mozart's *Lacrimosa*, Bach's double-violin concerto, or Rachmaninoff's *Vocalese* without being touched to the quick? Brahms, they say, used to sit at his piano composing and howling sometimes like a lost soul, as he heard the sounds produced by his almost-autonomous fingers. I do not suggest that music always has that effect upon people (hardly!), yet I've found that those profoundly endowed with musical intuition usually have an innate understanding of why the poet could speak of "The still, sad music of humanity."[62]

Moltmann, as I have noted, insists that the theology of the cross is the "key signature" of Christian theology. In my book *The Cross in Our Context*, I drew on the metaphor of major and minor harmonies in music and remarked that some people, hearing the typical themes and expressions of the *theologia crucis*, are likely to think it is all written in the minor key. Not incidentally, in view of the cultural comparison I ventured earlier, the most characteristic music of the Anglo-Saxon peoples draws heavily on the *major* keys. There are exceptions; perhaps the Welsh are the most prominent of these. (I once heard an accomplished English pianist and composer condescendingly remark of the Welsh and of other peoples whose preference for the minor harmonies is evident in their folk melodies that, of course, they are "children at heart.") Life, however (not only among earth's "children"), is often written in the minor key. The subliminally poignant music of life does not lend itself to once-for-all resolution by some resounding major chord. In any case, great music usually modulates between major and minor harmonies and involves contrapuntal progressions that do not easily complement one another. Interestingly, in view of the earlier references to contextuality, much symphonic and other music of our own time reflects discord, dissonance, and irresolution more conspicuously than it does their opposites.

Nothing in the realm of art guarantees that artists will be free of simplistic, premature, or even absurd miscalculations about life as soon as they move beyond the sphere of their art. (Consider Richard Wagner!) But if music, to speak only of that art, is combined with other influences—as it was in the case of Johann Sebastian Bach, an intuitive theologian of great sensitivity—it can and *must* call in question that within all of us that wants to embrace oversimplification and premature triumphs of the positive. It is not likely coincidental that the theologian who named the distinction between a *theologia crucis* that "calls the thing by its proper name" and the *theologia gloriae* that deceives was also a gifted musician.

Given these four components of my own spiritual journey and

others of a similar hue that I shall not name, I have frequently found myself at odds with the "official optimism" of my culture, especially its *religious* expressions. Again, I do not regard it as a virtue; I would never have chosen this path had I been asked. But from adolescence on, I have been incapable of assenting to any ideas about existence that asked me to let go of my innate sense of life's ambiguities and enigmas. It has always seemed to me that being a human being is a terribly demanding, if not impossible, form of creaturehood. I struggled in particular against the Christianity of my childhood and youth, which I felt depended for its credibility on a phenomenal blindness to reality and produced in its adherents the kind of moral self-righteousness that is attainable only by those apparently incapable of self-knowledge. I found myself—often to my own discontent—noticing the unacknowledged pride and self-satisfaction that the pious experienced on account of their "good deeds," which were usually paltry enough in themselves.

Christianity, in which I was reared, only became interesting and meaningful to me when I began to detect in it some undertone of truthfulness about the shadow side. The first book of the Bible that made it impossible for me ever again to dismiss that Holy Book was Ecclesiastes: "Vanity of vanities, saith the preacher, all is vanity. What profit hath a man of all his labour which he taketh under the sun?" (1:2-3 KJV). I felt I could trust a text that admitted so forthrightly the power of "the anxiety of meaninglessness and emptiness"[63] in human life and thought. So long as it could sustain that kind of forthrightness, I could begin slowly to trust as well the Bible's testimony to meaning and fulfillment.

And that, in a manner of speaking, is why I was led in time to explore at depth a theological tradition for which my own cultural background gave me little if any preparation.

This analysis of where I am now requires one further observation: While Anglo-Saxon thought and faith have pursued a rather one-sided if (by historical standards) *relatively* benign cultural and religious triumphalism, there has always been in our peculiar stream of Western civilization, particularly in imaginative literature, a countercultural awareness of the other side of things. And as the most conspicuous triumphs of the English-speaking world wane, some-times manifesting their tragic flaws at the height of their seeming successes, that other side has become more visible and vocal (in our films, for example). Maybe what the sensitive ones in Germanic cul-tures never could ignore—this older, premodern sense of life's abys-mal depths—can become part of what we need in these dominantly Anglo-Saxon societies to give us the courage to enter the dark age ahead that many fear[64]—to enter it and so, perhaps, chart its dark-ness with enough insight to help others live in it and even, hopefully, beyond it. A Christianity that remembers the cross of Jesus Christ and lives under it will not be out of place in such a context.

The Journey Ahead

The first two sections in this chapter required reflection on my personal journey. This third is less personal (though it is certainly not impersonal) because it concerns matters whose outcome remains to be seen—by me, I hope, in some at least anticipatory way, and certainly by all who care about the future of this wise and life-affirming tradition we call Judeo-Christian. In the latter half of one's eighth decade, one cannot assume that one's own journey will be extensive—though, if it is, one hopes to be up to it. But this title implies a journey that transcends my personal sojourn in time. I have understood this assignment as asking me to offer some assessment of what I think lies ahead for the Christian movement as a whole and for the region of particular concern and responsibility for me and most of my readers: the two northern nations of North America.

Journey is an excellent metaphor for a movement that understood itself—before its establishment—precisely as a people "of the way," en route, in transit. Perhaps the very first thing that needs to be said about the Christian future is that it will be and *must* be a rediscovery of this metaphor and an intentional, imaginative application of the metaphor to its own life. Like our parents in faith, we Christians all too soon exchanged tents for houses, the wilderness for the city. How very settled we have been—and for so long. We've practically lost the knack for travel.

But the One whom we try to follow when we are attentive to our calling is far ahead of us. He is already facing the dangers of the way that we are trying so hard to avoid. We shall not avoid them, in fact, no matter how preoccupied we become with our present in-house concerns—our pseudo-ecumenical squabbles, our struggle to survive economically without changing our "lifestyle," our escape into liturgy and "spirituality," our precious quest for "right doctrine," our vestigial moralism, and so forth. The *great* decisions we are going to have to make and will make—if not intentionally, then by default and through a sinful failure to read the signs of the times—concern problems and possibilities that are already clearly present before us. They become unavoidable as soon as we stick our noses outside the doors of our sanctuaries and see what is waiting for us there in the marketplace called world.

In this final section, I want to name and examine briefly five such areas of crucial decision making for the voyage ahead. On some of these five themes, I have already published a good deal; with others, I am only beginning to do some homework. I would be grateful to be given the time and health to investigate them further, but they are part of the theological and ecclesiastical agenda that has already been explored by some in the vanguard and must become the work of the entire Christian community.

MOVING BEYOND CHRISTENDOM

The first thing that must be said about the Christian future, surely, is that it will be—must be—a journey beyond Christendom. This is one of the subjects on which I have written rather extensively,[65] so I shall devote less space to it here than it deserves, but it certainly comes first.

Christendom—by which I mean the dominion not of the Christ but of the Christian religion in the Western world—has been in the process of ending for at least two centuries. The forces overthrowing the hegemony of the Christian religion in Europe and its satellites can be traced as far back as the breakdown of the medieval synthesis of faith and reason. But, more conspicuously, they made themselves felt in the Enlightenment of the eighteenth century and are punctuated politically by the French and (in some respects) the American revolutions. What we call secularism (a word invented in the mid-nineteenth century)[66] has been a long time working itself out, and it is not, after all, a very satisfactory alternative to religious faith. Most latter-day secularists are unhappy with their own outlook. Many, as the great Samuel Beckett said, are "mourning the death of God." The secular boasting of the eighteenth century gave way to the melancholy, romantic agnosticism of the nineteenth and then to the working despair and nihilism of the twentieth. From time to time, secular people try to reinvent some kind of spirituality (New Age seems largely an example) because it is not very comforting to see oneself—to see our entire species—alone and supposedly in charge of a universe that is (as Albert Camus believed and tried not to believe) basically indifferent to human pursuits. So the secularism that set in with the demise of Christendom and has affected all of us one way or another has its ups and downs. Sometimes, in the down periods, it calls upon religion again. And when history gets particularly bleak, as some believe it to be now, there is a kind of temporary rush on the churches, synagogues, mosques, and temples of the land.

Christians should not let this periodic resurgence of religion fool them into thinking that Christendom might not be over after all. Christendom—Christianity as the official and majority religion of a society, as the cult officially recognized by the governing powers—is largely a thing of the past. It lasted in an important but restricted area of the globe from the fourth until about the seventeenth century. Since then, it has been in various forms and degrees of decline.

I am speaking here quite explicitly of *Western* civilization. The Christian religion is growing at a spectacular rate in Africa, Asia, and Latin America.[67] The recent book by Philip Jenkins, a professor of history and religious studies at Pennsylvania State University, argues that Christendom is regrouping, as it were, in those three continents. Jenkins's book is even entitled *The Next Christendom*. In it, he states, "Within the next twenty-five years, the population of the world's Christians is expected to grow to 2.6 billion (making Christianity by far the world's largest faith). By 2025, 50 percent of the Christian population will be in Africa and Latin America, and another 17 percent will be in Asia."[68] I certainly do not doubt these statistics, but I question the spin that Professor Jenkins puts upon them. To call this expansion of the Christian religion in these continents "the next Christendom" is to place a qualitative interpretation upon them that is based on sheer quantity. Christendom, historically—Western Christendom—is not so named just because it accounted for a lot of people. Christendom refers to a whole political structure: the association of the Christian religion with the great powers of imperial civilizations. As I learned from my friend and former doctoral student Ishmael Noko, a native of Zimbabwe who has been the General Secretary of the World Lutheran Federation in Geneva for several years, what is happening in Africa is not "Christendom," because it has very little relation to political power. Another friend, theologian Russell Botman of South Africa, pointed out that the largest numbers of those who turn to Christianity in Africa are in fact the powerless, including many women.[69]

Above all, Christians *in the West* should not look to the growth of the Christian religion in these other places to avoid coming to terms with what has been happening in Europe, North America, Australia, New Zealand, and elsewhere for two centuries. Christendom as we have known it will not be "saved" by relocating elsewhere! As the most astute observers of the course of the Christian religion have observed for a long time (think of Kierkegaard), there was something questionable about the whole phenomenon of Christendom from the outset. Something vital was lost when Constantine and his successors invited the church to become chaplain to empire. And the salvation of Christianity is not to put the Humpty Dumpty of Christendom back together again, but to recover that something that was lost.

What was that? It was, if I may put it in a word, the capacity of the Christian gospel to befriend creation and all earth's creatures, including humankind. When Christianity allowed itself to become the darling of power structures, dominant races and classes, and established systems (and that is what Christendom is all about), it lost its capacity to be there for the whole, and especially those parts of the whole creaturely context that were victimized by the very power structures that the Christians were so keen to court.

I see the end of Christendom not as a tragedy, not as loss, not as something to mourn, but as opportunity. There are opportunities for genuine Christian witness that can be embraced only by a church that knows its existence is no longer guaranteed by convention, custom, or law, a church that is no longer part of the establishment. Disestablishment is not a fate that must be accepted; it is an opportunity that can be joyfully embraced. A church that is no longer simply part of the establishment—no longer the middle class at prayer, or at *something*—has the chance to be a prophetic alternative to the status quo. It is no longer under obligation to sanction the policies, values, and mores of the legislative and economic powers with which it has been associated in the past. The Church of Jesus Christ can be, in fact, far more vigilant for and responsible toward its host society—its whole society, not just the prosperous and powerful parts thereof—when it is distinct and distinguishable from the power structures of its society.

Instead of trying to protect our own most-favored status, instead of attempting to prolong Christendom by catering to the preferences of the policy-making classes of our society, Christian bodies in the West should actively embrace our de facto disestablishment. Instead of waiting for it to happen to us more and more conspicuously, as it surely will, we should take hold of the process of disestablishment and give it some definition, some positive direction. Let us deliberately disengage ourselves from the role of "culture religion" that we have been expected to play all these centuries—not to the end that we might become a ghetto or a holy sect, but in order that we might reengage our society from a position that is sufficiently different from our society to make some truly positive contribution to its welfare. For far too long, the churches have functioned chiefly to legitimate the dominant culture; the opportunity is there for us now to help to *transform* our culture. And it is a culture very badly in need of transformation!

HOSPITALITY TOWARD THE "OTHER"

Another factor that must concern anyone who as a Christian thinks of the journey ahead falls under the heading "religious plurality," an innocuous enough heading, as it has seemed, but one that becomes all too concrete in the rush and tumble of global events today. Throughout most of its history, the Christian religion has dealt with other religious faiths by ignoring them, trying to eradicate them, or reducing them to inferior and backward accounts of God, the world, and all things. None of these approaches can be tolerated today. We cannot ignore the others, as our forebears could; we live in a global village. We cannot engage in crusades, pogroms, and witch hunts against them (though the urge to do so still lingers in vociferous minorities among us, sadly). And neither can we settle the question of their existence by persuading ourselves that these other faiths are less advanced, less morally sound, less profound intellectually than ours. Most of us realize that all such judgments are made chiefly on the basis of very little real knowledge.

Very few of us, even among those who have been educated for ministry, were introduced at any depth to the study of other religions. The events beginning on September 11, 2001, have impressed on all thinking Christians the need for a more informed understanding of Islam at least; for many of us have been horrified by the manner in which (in the minds of so many of our fellow citizens) Islam has had to assume the blame for the actions of some who identify themselves as Muslims. We know how loudly we should ourselves object were Christianity to be defined by the actions of "Christo-fascists" (Soelle) or white supremacists and other distortions of our faith. If anything at all that is good can come out of the ruins of the twin towers of Manhattan, it would have to be a new determination on the part of Western Christians to acquaint themselves as deeply and sympathetically as possible with the tenets of Islam. That at least—for a start!

Already more than forty years ago, my fellow Canadian, the late Wilfred Cantwell Smith, founder of the comparative religion departments at both McGill and Harvard, wrote the following words in a little book called *The Faith of Other Men*:

> No longer are people of other persuasions peripheral or distant, the ideal curiosities of travelers' tales. The more alert we are, and the more involved in life, the more we are finding that they are our neighbours, our colleagues, our competitors, our fellows. Confucians and Hindus, Buddhists and Muslims are with us not only in the United Nations but down the street. Increasingly, not only is our civilization's destiny affected by their actions; but we drink coffee with them personally as well.

I personally do not expect many conversions from one tradition to another . . . Yet we may all confidently expect increasing encounters among the varying traditions; and consequent ferment within each group. It will become increasingly apparent, and is already essentially true, that to be a Christian in the modern world, or a Jew, or an agnostic, is to be so in a society in which other people, intelligent, devout, and righteous, are Buddhists, Muslims, Hindus.[70]

The very first requirement that such a situation places upon serious Christians is that they must become informed about these other faith traditions—a task that surely has many facets, including the study of the texts of other faiths and listening to those who are best able to articulate their faith. We should certainly not judge other faiths by listening only to their most questionable advocates or by absolutizing our own prejudices.

Scholars talk about three attitudes toward religious plurality: exclusivism, inclusivism, and pluralism.

Exclusivism

Exclusivism is the approach of those whose commitment to one religion is such that it prevents them from any kind of openness to the others. They feel they possess or are uniquely in touch with ultimate truth, so any other claim to truth is excluded a priori. This attitude can be assumed by Christians only when they distort their own faith. As Christians, we do not *possess* the Truth. The Truth to which faith orients us cannot be possessed. Jesus did not say to his disciples, "Here's the truth, class: write it down, and don't change one word." He said, according to John's account, "I am the Truth" (John 14:6). This was not a statement of the ultimate in egoism, but a way of saying that the truth is a living reality, an *incarnate* Word. As such, the Truth with which Christians have to do can only be lived; it cannot be had.

If we start with that realization, we can never approach others as if we had what they do not and could not have. Jesus' Truth is not have-able! Our human tendency to engage in that kind of presumption (and how very human it is—how unredeemedly human) has been and is being taken from us by the very Spirit who illumines us. In exchange, the divine Spirit offers us a new modesty, a new readiness to listen. As Karl Barth, reputedly the most "dogmatic" theologian of his age, put it, Christian theology is "the most modest science," and its modesty is not just a matter of bourgeois niceness, but a consequence of close attention to the object of this "science," who is no object but a living Subject.[71]

Inclusivism

The approach to other religions taken by many liberal Christians is inclusivism. This approach is certainly more compatible with the Christ about whom one reads in the New Testament, who opens himself to all sorts and conditions of persons, than is exclusivism. If I have to choose between the two, I shall choose inclusivism right away. But I do not think these two limit the choices. There is a tendency in the inclusivist approach to include without scrutiny, without asking any questions, and really without paying much attention to those included. It can be a very lazy attitude, a general openness to everyone and everything—very magnanimous, very nice, but finally not as loving as it would like to think itself. It welcomes difference but too often without noticing what is different about it—and without allowing it to *be* different.

Pluralism

The approach to religious diversity taken mainly by intellectuals is pluralism. It finds truths in all positions, but (this is my complaint about it) the pluralist remains rather condescendingly above all specific religions—above their messy particularity and concreteness, above their petty squabbles. Christians can certainly learn from philosophic pluralism, but I do not see how Christians can as such *be* pluralists. If I am committed to Christian faith or to any other particular faith, I cannot easily abandon that commitment in favor of a detachment from *all* particular faith traditions, including my own.

Hospitable Christianity

An alternative approach to religious plurality that I have tried to explore a little and that many others are now writing about in creative ways is called *hospitality*. Hospitality has the advantage of being a biblical category, indeed, a very important one. Moreover, hospitality informs also—and centrally—our two sister Abrahamic faiths, Judaism and Islam. While hospitality toward the other contains elements of the three alternatives I have just described, it differs from each of them. Unlike pluralism, hospitality does assume a particular faith commitment, whether Christian or other. Unlike liberal inclusivism, it does not include blindly or simply on principle, but it invites dialogue; it wants really to get to know the other, to discover points of convergence and points of divergence. Above all, it wants to find ways in which all sincere religions can work together for the well-being of the world (and there are many such ways). This openness, this hospitality should never be thought just a virtue that Christians may or may not develop; it is a consequence of their faith. For the basic assumption of this hospitality is that the real host is not itself, not Christianity as such, not the church, but the One who has so graciously received us and who from the start warned us that He has sheep who are not of this fold.

Hospitable Christianity is not shocked or surprised at the multicultural, multifaith context in which it now finds itself at the outset of the twenty-first century. It does not hanker after a past in which it was virtually alone, albeit in a limited portion of the earth, in its quest for the souls of people and nations. Religious plurality, after all, is not just a contemporary phenomenon; it was the original condition of the very first churches. If we take the Bible as normative for faith, we must recognize plurality of religion as the *normal* context of the Christian community and mission. By biblical criteria, the Christian hegemony that prevailed in the West throughout the centuries of Christendom must now be thought abnormal. Christians at the beginning, before Constantine, and Christians now and henceforth, after the Constantinian era, exist in a world where there are many alternatives to the Christian account of reality. In some of those alternatives, Christians may discover, as Paul did, parallel teachings and ethical concerns. With others they will find little common ground. But the biblical law of hospitality to the stranger holds in *all* such encounters, and if we Christians cannot practice this hospitality quite concretely in our very diverse, increasingly diverse global culture, we shall have failed at the most basic level of obedience to the Christ: the law of love.

JESUS

My third area of concern as I consider the Christian journey in the decades ahead is, in one word, Jesus. Jesus and our attitude toward Jesus are, of course, the point to which we must come in our life vis-à-vis other faiths. Even where the other two Abrahamic faiths are concerned, perhaps especially with them, Jesus as the Christ is the point of great contention. What our theological forebears named "the scandal of particularity" is even more present with us today than it was with Barth and Tillich and the others.

From one perspective, the crucified one is (in Paul's term) a "scandal" (*skandalon*) because of his particularity and his suffering, but Jesus is also our best entrée to a meaningful dialogue with others. He is, as I put it in my description of hospitable Christianity, the unseen but very real Host in our attempts at hospitality toward the other.

Particularity as Necessity

Certainly, Jesus stands at the very center of Christian faith. Our faith is Christocentric. One can only claim Christianity for a confession of faith if Jesus Christ is at its center. As we affirm, the most characteristic form of Christian prayer is "through Jesus Christ, our Lord." So, yes, this is very particularistic. A particular historical figure, the subject of particular events and particular places, is the foundational ground of our faith, and we cannot and dare not forget this.

But is this, after all, such a scandalous thing? Is there *any* faith that does not have its particular entrée to the ultimate? Judaism, which may come closest to being pure monotheism, defines God through particular events, figures, and texts—through particular core events, especially the exodus, in which the divine will is revealed, and through a particular tradition of law, wisdom, prophecy, and poetry. Islam points to an utterly transcendent deity, Allah. But it does so through Muhammad, his very particular prophet, and through a book, the Koran, which Islam regards with even greater solemnity than most Christians regard the Bible. A rather eclectic religion like Baha'i, which has seemed to some of our contemporaries to avoid this need for particulars, makes much of the figure of Bahā Allāh.[72]

In short, the truth is surely that any faith, or indeed any philosophy that wants to have some access to the Ultimate, can have it only by passing through the lens of some particular mediator, some special mediating experience, some specific set of circumstances or ideas or texts. There is, in fact, no way of moving *directly* to the Absolute, for we ourselves are particular, finite, historical creatures. The universal is always approached through the particular.

So when Christians picture God and all things eternal by reference to the particular being named Jesus, they are not doing something unusual. In principle, they are doing just what everybody else does who wishes to feel some proximity to the eternal: namely, they perceive the eternal through special attention to some illuminating temporal reality.

Opening the Door to Dialogue

The second stage in this argument is where we Christians have to watch our step. Suppose we convince others that our adherence to the particular called Jesus is a perfectly reasonable thing to do—something that all believers of every sort do, one way or another. The next question we have to ask ourselves is, What sort of particular is this? What is this Jesus like, and how does he function for us? Especially, how does he help us in our attempts to relate to others—or does he perhaps hinder us in that attempt?

We know from ordinary, everyday experience that particulars function for people in different ways. There are men (I am told) who will not allow their wives or sweethearts to look sideways at another male. There are mothers and fathers in every school who are so persuaded of the uniqueness and superiority of their child that they see all other children as a great intellectual handicap, a mass of mediocrity. Well, and there are Christians too (are there not?) who see "their" Jesus as demanding of them such exclusive attention that they are effectively robbed of outgoingness, even of the ordinary human decency they might have had as a natural quality, apart from their religious fervor. Watching such Christians and listening to them, one often wonders, "Mightn't they have been better people without 'their' Jesus?" Unfortunately, these tend to be the noisiest and most noticeable Christians in the North American scene. They are so committed to their "Jesus" that they'd have had, surely, a very rough time following the *biblical* Jesus around, as he opened himself to all those prostitutes and tax collectors and persons of other religious persuasion with whom he engaged in intimate relations.

Still, particulars may and often do function quite differently. They do not close us off, but open us to the other. I know a man, for instance, who at a rather late age managed to have four children, all of them indubitably unique and wondrous. Through those children, he learned to develop a new sensitivity to the whole world of children and so (as I remarked in the first section) began to think about the future well beyond my own likely participation in time. And I know a man who, because he was loved by a very particular woman, learned despite his own no doubt innate male chauvinism to become more sensitive toward all woman. That particular woman did not say (as women sometimes do say to their mates), "You belong to me! Watch it!" Instead, she in effect said in a thousand little ways, mostly unspoken, "I am a woman. Get to know me. Half the world is more like me than it is like you. See the world through the eyes of a human being who is able to bear and nurture babies. Get to know her suffering and her hope."

Yes, and I also know a man who, because he felt and feels himself to be encountered by the spirit of Jesus, has through trial and error learned to be far more open to human beings generally, religious and irreligious, male and female, white and brown and tan, rich and poor, straight and gay—far more open to persons of every sort and condition than he would or could ever have been apart from this encounter with the Crucified One.

I know this man rather well. I am he.

What I mean to say in this personal way is that *if* we Christians honestly and humbly position ourselves within the particular tradition handed over to us, *if* we do not turn that tradition into something that it is not (such as a Bible that is assumed to be literally infallible, doctrine that imagines it has captured Almighty God in little dogmas, a Holy Spirit who is chained and shackled to our own petty preferences and prejudices, and a Jesus Christ who functions for us like a jealous husband or a spoiled child, demanding exclusive attention to himself, that is, to what we've reduced him to), *if* we try to live intelligently and faithfully within our own living christological tradition, then we shall find ourselves being carried bodily and spiritually and intellectually into the great wide world in ways we never dreamed possible or desirable.

The confession of faith in the triune God of our tradition, when it is understood as something greater than the mere *profession* of dogma, is not a barrier to meaningful dialogue and solidarity with persons of other faiths and unfaiths. To the contrary, it is the very means by which such dialogue and solidarity are sustained. To live, think, speak, and act as disciples of Jesus, the Christ, in our kind of post-Christendom, religiously diverse, and culturally complex world—scandalously exclusive as such a confession may seem—is to be led into the most inclusive, unbounded human and creaturely communality anyone can imagine. If Jesus as he was and is and will be is our Guide into the great immensity that is life in this world, we shall find ourselves beckoned into places and causes and relationships whose breadth and scope will always astonish us, sometimes scare us, and in the end liberate us from the narrowness and provincialism of our own inherited values and destinies.

THE HUMAN VOCATION IN THE MIDST OF CREATION

As I consider the Christian future, I am also concerned with the relation between the human species and the rest of creation. This relation, it seems to me, is the scene of the greatest ethical questions today and will be increasingly so tomorrow. We have hardly begun to sort it out or even to take in the great scope of it. We seem to be able to deal only with the *effects* of the problem, not its root nature or cause. Its most far-reaching cause is clearly an immense distortion in the way that human beings (especially among the possessing peoples of the earth) have construed their relationship with the natural order. But let me be concrete.

For the past forty years, my family and I have spent our summers on a small island in the north channel of Lake Huron. The water level in the Great Lakes has dropped more than a meter in the last two or three years. We have a lot more island now than when we bought that property forty years ago—and we don't want more!

The five Great Lakes of North America account for 20 percent of the planet's freshwater. Ninety-nine percent of that water is glacial; it was deposited up there, between our two countries, by the last great ice age—a gift of divine providence if ever there was one!

But so polluted have these waters been over the past decades that my family, living at the northernmost shore of Lake Huron, not even in the industrial south, must purchase its drinking water from a local outlet in the town nearby and carry it across to the island. Everybody in that area asks, "What has happened to the big lake? Why is its water no longer drinkable? And what happened to nearly four feet of water over all that immense surface?" Some say the levels of the lake are cyclical, which may be partly true. Others say there has not been enough rain, which may be partly true. But many say that if you double and quadruple the size of the great cities that rely on the Great Lakes for their water, and if you add to that the indeterminate increase in human demands for water (all those lawns that must be kept green, for instance), and if you add to this the seemingly bottomless pit of agricultural development such as the Ohio Valley and similar projects, then you will deplete these glacial deposits inevitably and perhaps forever. There are large freshwater lakes on earth that have already dried up.

The latest theory, outlined in a scientific article in the *Canadian Geographic*, is that the water from the largest lake of them all (the combined lakes of Huron and Michigan) is being drained out through the Saint Clair River, which has been dredged ever deeper, much deeper than international treaties allow, thus creating a flow-off of glacial waters through Lakes Erie and Ontario, thence into the Saint Lawrence River, and out into the sea—and so lost forever as freshwater.[73]

No new water is being made. All the water there is going to be in Earth's biosphere is already here. For better or worse, however, new people are being made, and many of these people have been conditioned to have huge appetites where water consumption is concerned.

Most of us already know this kind of analysis, yet we do very, very little to alter our overuse and misuse of the limited resources of our planet. We are so enthralled by the soteriology of technology that we assume all such potential problems as arise from nature's limits will be met, in due course, by new technologies that will replace the old. In short, we have shown ourselves completely unwilling to adjust our lifestyle to conform to the realities of our environment. We continue to see ourselves not only at the center of the natural order but above it. The modern vision of human mastery over nature still inspires our whole civilizational project. Thomas Hobbes, writing in the seventeenth century, still speaks for us today: "She [Nature] is no mystery, for she worketh by motion and geometry . . . We can chart these motions. Feel then, as if you live in a world which can be measured, weighed and mastered, and *confront it with audacity*."[74]

Fortunately, there has been in our time a strong protest against this "audacity." As I indicated in my first section, environmental consciousness as it first came to my attention through the scientists working in the University of Saskatchewan has long been a factor in my theological thought. For practical purposes, I am with the protesting element, even when they are extreme, for they represent by far the less-powerful voice in this struggle. Christians in Canada and the United States, both of which countries are far behind Europe in addressing these problems, must exercise a strong critical vigilance against the failure of our nations fully to embrace international decisions like the Kyoto Protocol (though Canada, thankfully, has done so now formally, if only we can follow through). The only thing that prevents our societies from adopting such minimal changes as Kyoto calls for is our corporate desire to maintain the status quo. We simply do not want to change anything about our "way of life." If you stand at a bus stop in any large city in North America and watch the steady stream of automobiles, most of them ferrying only a single human being to some likely inconsequential destination at the fastest possible speed, and if, as you watch, you realize that you are also breathing in the fumes that no "advanced technology" can extricate from these gasoline-driven vehicles, and if you notice that the line for the bus contains mainly women, people of color, and youngsters—and all this in a city (like mine) with excellent public transportation, then you may well wonder whether anything at all can be done about the increasingly alarming fact of global warming.

Christians have a unique and nuanced position to contribute to this debate, and it is not quite compatible with either the capitalist-industrialist approach or the more radical forms of the protest against the status quo. Among the latter, the impression is too often created that the human species is so problematic that the only real solution to the degradation of the natural order would be humankind's drastic reduction or even its graceful disappearance. There is a famous statement by the Harvard scientist E. O. Wilson, expert on biodiversity, to the effect that if the human species disappeared, the Earth would flourish, whereas if the ant species disappeared, there would be catastrophe.[75] I do not doubt the truth of this generalization; it seems, unfortunately, all too accurate. But should the ethical conclusion of such pithy generalizations be that all who care about the fate of the Earth ought actively to engage in causing humans to "disappear"? Even such a ridiculous conclusion would demonstrate that human beings must be significantly different from other species. For, notwithstanding the example of the lemmings, the nonhuman species seem magnificently to illustrate the law of self-preservation. What species other than the human would even contemplate moving out of the way so that the rest of nature could flourish?

Yes, Christianity does affirm the specialness of the human creature. There can be no doubt about that. But this specialness, in the biblical tradition, is not reckoned in terms of innate value or in an odious comparison with other, nonhuman species; it is reckoned in terms of the *vocation* of the human creature among the creatures. The difference of the human from the others—including its powers of rationality, will, dexterity, and so forth—is not regarded in biblical literature as valuable merely in itself, but as the means of enabling this creature to play a particular role in the great and diverse community of creation. Biblically, that role is described in many ways: the human as priest, as poet, as seer, as representative. But I have found that the most timely biblical metaphor on which Christians may draw for their particular way of regarding this relation in our own time is the metaphor of the steward.[76]

There is, you know, an important polemic in this seemingly pretty metaphor: if you say that the human creature is steward, you are saying at the same moment, "Yes, steward, *not owner*, not master, not sovereign." That over which this stewardly creature is called to its vocation of tender care belongs to Another: "The earth is the Lord's, and the fullness thereof" (Psalm 24:1 KJV). This critical dimension of the idea of stewardship—especially in a society like ours, which tends to take human *management* of everything for granted—must not be forgotten. (I was annoyed when the translators of the New Revised Standard Version of the Bible took it upon themselves to drop the ancient term *steward* from the older translations and use the modern term *manager*. In our context, manager is clearly a status concept. The biblical steward, as in Jesus' parables, is by no manner or means the CEO of creation.) The steward reports to Another and lives and works within laws and limits set by that Other. This speaks directly against the idea of human mastery and autonomy—against the "audacity" of sinful Homo sapiens, so-called.

But the steward metaphor contains a constructive as well as a critical dimension. The steward in biblical narrative is (yes!) *accountable*, but the biblical steward is also *responsible*. The human steward is no better than other creatures: he or she is a creature among creatures, a servant among servants. We share the same lot as all the others: mortality, finitude, a certain destiny within whose boundaries there can be some flexibility. Only it is our burden (a necessary burden, for the sake of our vocation) that we know this about our condition. Our difference from the other creatures is not in *being* but in *calling*, vocation. We are given a particular responsibility. We are to represent, in the midst of the creation, the gracious, caring, suffering Creator—yes, the *suffering* Creator; for here is where stewardship theology also must emerge out of the theology of the cross. Our so-called human dominion in creation has nothing at all in common with the "audacious" dominion of a Caesar or a Napoleon—or, for that matter, General Motors. Ours is to represent the dominion of the one we designate *Dominus*, our "Lord"—that is, the dominion of the shepherd who lays down his life for the sheep, for his friends.[77]

It is, of course, very difficult to maintain this nuanced Christian position of the relation between humankind and otherkind in our sort of society today, because the argument has been cast in the form of an ongoing tussle between extremes: the technocrats and the extreme ecologists. Christians ought to work on the side of the protesting environmentalists because they are the weaker in this struggle, but Christians cannot be satisfied with either a technocratic elevation of the human above all the rest or with a demotion of the human to the status of a merely problematic element. Somehow, despite this difficulty, we must learn how to communicate our understanding of this relationship. It will help to do so if we are ready to discover in other religious faiths understandings of this relationship that are parallel with our own. Many Christians have felt that we have much to learn from Buddhism here. Unless we work at a new understanding of the human/extrahuman relation (which is also a very old understanding of this relation), we leave the future to conflicting ideologies of the extreme.

A THINKING FAITH

My final word on the matter of our journey into the future has to do with the necessity of our becoming and being a *thinking* faith. There is a problem today that is found not only in Christianity but in most of the religions, as well as in many nonreligious ideologies. I will call this the problem of certitude. Its corrective is the importance of Christianity's being a thinking faith—and, more specifically, the importance of doubt in the life of faith.

The people who attacked the United States on September 11, 2001, were apparently inspired by absolute certainty with respect to their cause. They found that certainty in their religious belief. Their religion functioned for them as an antidote against all self-doubt, all consciousness of the limitations of knowledge, all awareness of the precariousness of human judgment. That religion was Islam—at least, according to their own account. But it could just as well have been an ultraconservative Judaism, or undiluted and militant capitalism, or any number of other faiths or ideologies. It could just as easily have been right-wing Christianity. No one religion, and not religion as a whole, has a monopoly on what (for want of a better word) we call fundamentalism. Fundamentalism, whatever the origins of the term, has come to mean a position of such exactness and certitude that those embracing it—or, more accurately, those embraced *by* it—feel themselves delivered from all the relativities, uncertainties, indefiniteness, and transience of human existence. They are provided, they feel, with a firm foundation—a *fundamentum*—greater than their own finitude, greater than any observations of any of the sciences, greater than the collective wisdom of the race.

I think we should not feel that this phenomenon is simply incomprehensible, a complete aberration. We all, as humans, fear uncertainty, long for certitude, and want to be surrounded and embraced by some system of meaning that will support and uphold us in our self-doubt. Moreover, the more chaotic and uncertain existence becomes, the more societies are gripped by fear, "future shock," and unknown terror, the more easily and naturally we are drawn to such systems. As Karen Armstrong writes in her splendid study *The Battle for God*:

> During the middle of the 20th Century, fundamentalists in all three of the monotheistic faiths were beginning to retreat from mainstream society [and, she might have added, from mainstream religion] to create countercultures that reflected the way they thought things

ought to be. They were not simply withdrawing out of pique, but were often impelled to do so by horror and fear. It is important that we understand the dread and anxiety that is at the heart of the fundamentalist vision, because only then will we begin to comprehend its passionate rage, its frantic desire to fill the void with certainty, and its conviction of ever-encroaching evil.[78]

At its best, biblical religion (at least in its Jewish and Christian appropriation; I do not yet know enough about Islam to speak intelligently for that faith, but my scholarly Islamic friends assure me that this is true of Islam as well) counters this altogether human need for certitude in two ways. First, it simply refuses to offer such certitude, and this refusal is not once for all, but an ongoing refusal. The myth of the Tower of Babel (Genesis 11) may be the best illustration of this. It is precisely out of their anxious quest for security and ultimacy that the people depicted as frantically building this city and this tower went about their attempts. Their aim is frustrated, rejected, refused, confused—and by the very God whose power and absoluteness they wanted to get hold of. This refusal of the "religious" temptation to acquire finality—refusal that is confirmed over and over again in biblical narrative and in countless ways—is, in fact, the first thing that humanity has to learn. Such security, such permanency, such finality simply does not belong to the human condition, whether in its "fallen" or its "created" state. And, as I tried to show in the second section, it is a lie—a piece of the theology of glory—whenever that kind of finality is offered as though it were possible. It is the same lie that Luther saw in his critique of religious triumphalism in general, for it is the essence of that theology to court that lie in particular.

But the God of biblical faith is merciful. God does not meet our need for security only with a refusal and rebuff. God offers us an alternative to certitude. It is called trust. God reveals Godself as one who may be trusted. Sight, or the kind of finality that sight seems to make possible, is not given. But faith is possible. This is behind Paul's recurring distinction between faith and sight.[79] God does not *give us* the Truth, yet God lets the Truth live among us, incarnate—

lets us glimpse enough of God's living Truth that we may learn the courage to live despite our real vulnerability, impermanence, and littleness. Certitude is denied; confidence is made possible. Consider that word: *confidence*. Literally, in the Latin, it means living with (*con*) faith (*fide*).

Now, faith is a living thing—it is a category of the present. It is not a once-for-all accomplishment. It is not a possession, like a Visa card, that some have and others don't. It is an ongoing response to God, to the world, to life. It is therefore a matter of decision—taken not once, but over and over again, and in the presence of much evidence to the contrary.

Because faith involves decision, and indeed *is* decision (the decision to trust), it necessarily involves its antithesis, doubt. And, like Tillich,[80] I do not mean just intellectual doubts, but existential doubt, the kind of doubt that wonders, "Dare I really trust this One?" "A faith that does not doubt," said Unamuno, "is a dead faith."[81] "Faith and doubt," wrote the late Jewish scholar Pinchas Lapide, "run like twin threads crosswise throughout the whole history of Israel."[82] Faith and doubt are opposites, true, though, as I observed in the second section, it would be better to call them polarities, like the positive and negative poles in electricity. They need one another, because neither can be what it is and do what it does without the other. Faith keeps doubt from becoming mere cynicism and nihilism; doubt keeps faith from becoming smug, routine, presumptuous—"dead faith."

Judaism may have understood this dialectic better than Christianity has. Christianity has tended to routinize faith or translate it into propositional form—partly, I suspect, because Christianity has so consistently functioned as religious establishment. Establishments need certitude. Judaism, which always had to exist on the move—a journey that seemed never to end in arriving—tends to understand faith in more existential or dramatic-narrative terms, the terms of the Scriptures. Think of the Psalms, with their recurring expressions of doubt and lamentation. One writer, in a selection of "the best contemporary Hebrew writing," cunningly characterizes this dialectic of doubt and faith in Jewish faith as follows: "It would not be possible for them *not* to believe; even though, generally speaking, they believe with perfect faith. This is a Jewish trait, too, a very Jewish trait, to believe with burning faith of all the heart and all the soul, and yet *somewhat* not to believe, the least little bit, and to let this tiny bit be . . . decisive!"[83]

Classical Protestantism, too (in at least one of its dimensions), understood the positive role of doubt in the life of faith. Sometimes, reading the Reformers and trying to follow their often tortuous explanations of doctrine, one has the impression, "Heavens! These Protestants sure do not believe easily!" No wonder Hans-Joachim Iwand called doubting Thomas *der erste Protestant*[84]—the first Protestant. Old-fashioned Protestants, in contrast with the "true believers" of popular electronic forms of what is called Protestantism, accept so little at face value, on the authority of the authorities. They don't even accept the claims of their darling book, the Bible, without a lot of earnest soul-searching. They want to *understand* everything. They even think ordinary people capable of understanding; that's why they put so much emphasis on preaching and Christian education. They mistrust ancient systems and conventions. They want to get back to the basics, they say, but compared with the fundamentalists with their five fundamentals, the Reformers argue a good deal about what really is basic. True, the Scriptures are, but they have to be interpreted. "The Bible," Luther was fond of saying, "has a wax nose"; you can twist it whichever way you want! In the end, these reforming Christians seem to regard as ultimate only the authority of the One who is above all the provisional authorities—their own included.

That, in Tillich's view (and mine), is the very heart of what he called "the Protestant principle": Nothing finite should be granted the authority of the Infinite. Nothing relative should be granted the authority of the Absolute.[85] So, at the heart of our Protestant beginnings, there is a strong protest against the phenomenon we now call "true belief." Certitude. A lovely statement of Luther is reported by Martin E. Marty: "When [Luther's] friend Justus Jonas lifted up St. Paul as a paradigm [of unwavering faith], Luther blurted out: 'I don't think Paul believed as firmly as he talks. I cannot believe as firmly, either, as I can talk and write about it.'"[86] But, of course, this kind of honesty and the theological insight that made it possible were countered within later Protestantism itself by its need to defend itself against Catholic and sectarian challenges and, simply, by the all-too-human need to seem right.

Today, the remnants of classical Protestantism are hard-pressed to recover the original and authentic Protestant sense of the existential, dialogical, and ongoing character of faith. They are even hard-pressed to present Christian faith as a *thinking* faith. The most successful versions of Christianity in the world today—particularly on this continent of ours—are those, it seems, that help people turn off their minds in favor of complete and unclouded certitude. In an age of covert and therefore all the more insidious despair and unknowing, there is a large market for liberation from any kind of sustained and serious thought. If you can tell people what they should believe and do, think and feel and wish for, and do it with televisible panache, you will not lack for a congregation!

But if the journey ahead is to have any real continuity with the great moments of our Christian past, we are going to have to recover the living quality of faith as a thinking faith that dialogues openly with its opposite. We must not allow the Christian faith to serve the simplistic and (as we should now know) the inevitably dangerous ends of fundamentalist religion. That would be a terrible betrayal of what is best and brightest in the tradition of Jerusalem. As Barbara Brown Taylor has written in a recent article for the *Christian Century*, commenting on the fascinating idea of the medieval thinker Nicholas of Cusa that true Christianity is "learnedly ignorant":

> In Nicholas's scheme, the dumbest people in the world are those who think they know. Their certainty about what is true not only pits them against each other; it also prevents them from learning anything new. This is truly dangerous knowledge. For they do not know that they do not know, and their *unlearned* ignorance keeps them in the dark about most things that matter.[87]

∾

With this thought, I end this chapter on one theologian's journey. However and whenever my own journey ends, the journey of the great ship of faith goes on. My hope for the Christian future is this: I hope we can embark on the future with the confidence of the learnedly ignorant. I hope we can avoid the certitude of those who "do not know that they do not know." I hope we can be a community of thinking faith and of faithful thinking.

With God's help, it can be done!

CHAPTER THREE

Stewards of the Mysteries of God:

Preserving Classical Protestant Theology

> This is how one should regard us, as servants of Christ and stewards of the mysteries of God.
>
> *—1 Corinthians 4:1* RSV

The vocation to theology applies not only to individual theologians, but to the church as a community of theological discourse. In the United States and Canada today, no work of corporate theology is more important than that of preserving the rightful heritage of Protestantism.

Protestantism—meaning classical Protestantism, the Protestantism that traces itself to the Reformation of the sixteenth century without being slavishly bound to its expressions half a millennium ago—as I see it is in trouble. One aspect of the trouble can be observed quantitatively, statistically. The newly published *Encyclopedia of Protestantism* (a four-volume publication containing, by the way, no article on Protestant-inspired theology of stewardship) in its article "Statistics" presents a rather glowing account of the situation that can sound like a veritable success story with its heading "Protestants and Catholics Each Reach 1.5 Billion."[1] But when you examine the fine print, you can easily detect the flaw by which success stories quantitatively told are nearly always marred. The Protestantism that accounts for by far the greater share of this figure is what the encyclopedia calls "wider" Protestantism, as distinct from "core" Protestantism. This so-called wider Protestantism (we are informed) includes everybody who is not Roman Catholic or Eastern Orthodox but claims a Christian heritage. It includes, that is to say, a great deal of religious teaching and practice that has little or nothing to do with the Protestantism that came out of the sixteenth-century Reformation.

The great trouble in which classical Protestantism finds itself, however, cannot be glimpsed quantitatively, for it is a qualitative matter. Its problems are more conspicuous in developed societies like ours than in the newer churches of the Southern Hemisphere. Statistics can pinpoint some of its consequences, but they cannot get at the deeper matter of causation. For instance, it is common knowledge that conservative, biblicist, and fundamentalist forms of Christianity in North America have surpassed the growth and influence of the old "mainline" Protestant denominations. In the *Encyclopedia of Protestantism*'s article on Protestantism in Canada, which I find more honest than most such analyses, John G. Stackhouse concludes, "The general picture [at the turn of the century] was simply one of the increasing marginalization of Canadian Protestantism and of Christianity in general," even including the "relative success story of the evangelicals."[2]

Statistics will confirm that so-called true-believing forms of Protestantism have been particularly conspicuous in U.S.-American life, not least of all in the arena of politics, but they will not tell us what sort of Christianity this allegedly successful Protestantism is, nor why it appeals to a frightened public, nor how it stands vis-à-vis Protestant origins and the evolution of Protestantism. Nor will such analyses convey to us very much about the causes of the diminishment of the formerly most "established" churches in the United States and Canada. For instance, they will not help us understand the factors that have brought about our loss of nerve, our failure to educate our laity beyond the most rudimentary clichés of the tradition (if that), our assumption that we could carry on business as usual long after the whole Constantinian framework of our culture-religion had collapsed, and so forth. Statistics will not show how predictable it ought to have been decades ago that the automatic churchgoing of yesteryear would disappear as soon as the social structures and public moods that held it in place had been altered, as they were (vastly), nor how, in consequence, an alert Protestantism ought to have been working long ago to articulate for itself the "reason for the hope that is in us" (1 Peter 3:15 KJV).

In short, statistics will not demonstrate that the primary cause of the humiliation of classical Protestantism on this continent has been the failure of these old denominations to be "stewards of the mysteries of God" (1 Cor 4:1) as those mysteries have been testified to in the traditions of the Reformation and its faithful interpretation in the best scholarship of the past four or five centuries.

Perhaps it is already too late to prevent the further erosion of the old Protestant churches on this continent. Frankly, as an ecumenical Christian who is quite prepared to spend his life in the multicultural and religiously pluralistic society that is our present social context, I am not overly anxious about the fate of specific denominations or even about the specific organizational form of a Christianity calling itself Protestant. But I am concerned that what the struggles of the Reformation produced by way of a better expression of biblical faith should not be lost to the world. And I am concerned that something might come to be and perhaps flourish that calls itself Protestant yet in essence has very little to do with that classical Protestant heritage and may in fact represent religious and moral assumptions antithetical to that heritage. I am concerned, too, that that heritage should not be reduced to the kind of traditional*ism* that is nothing but "the dead faith of the living." Stewarding the Protestant tradition means listening attentively to "the living faith of the dead" so that the present community of discipleship may find its way into the future.[3]

To do that, the community must always adapt the lessons it learns from the past to the realities of the present, many of which are entirely new and would not have been understood by the fathers and mothers of Protestant beginnings. Therefore, when I speak about "classical" Protestantism, I do not mean a Protestantism that is content simply to perpetuate the teachings of Martin Luther, John Calvin, Huldrych Zwingli, John Knox, and the others. Rather, I mean a Protestantism that has so absorbed those foundational traditions that it is able to deconstruct and reconstruct them in the light of the exigencies of the present and impending future.

It is no doubt foolhardy to attempt to name those foundational traditions; any such naming will involve a subjective element and leave many questions unanswered, particularly when it must be brief. Unless one risks such specificity, however, the entire subject will be left at the level of generalities and vague exhortations. So, comforted by the proverb that fools rush in where angels fear to tread (which has to be the motto of Christian theology done under the conditions of history), I shall take the risk of identifying what I regard as six paramount emphases of the Protestant tradition that we are called to steward. Each one of them, in typical Reformation fashion, is set over against temptations inhering in the principle under discussion—a temptation whose power is amply and perpetually demonstrated in the actual history of Protestantism.

CHRISTOCENTRISM (*CONTRA* CHRISTOMONISM)

The first principle of classical Protestantism that must be named is, of course, its being centered in Jesus, the Christ. Paul Tillich speaks as a true Protestant when he writes:

> Christianity is what it is through the affirmation that Jesus of Nazareth, who has been called "the Christ," is actually the Christ, namely, he who brings the new state of things, the New Being. Whenever the assertion that Jesus is the Christ is maintained, there is the Christian message; wherever this assertion is denied, the Christian message is not affirmed.[4]

The *per Christum solum* ("through Christ alone") of the Reformers precedes and gives the rationale for all their other priorities: *sola gratia, sola fide, sola Scriptura* (grace alone, faith alone, scripture alone).

But this positive affirmation of the centrality of Jesus Christ in classical Protestantism must not be turned into a myopic spiritual singularity and exclusivity that rules out any concentration other than a formulary, doctrinaire Christology. The temptation inherent in Christianity's concentration on the Christ is the reduction of Christocentrism to Christomonism. And (according to H. Richard Niebuhr, for instance), that is precisely what North American Christianity has done. In defiance both of historic Christology and the doctrine of the Trinity, it has opted for a "divine" Christ whose humanity is strictly formal and, accordingly, for what Niebuhr called "unitarianism of the second person of the Trinity."[5] Perhaps the Reformers did not guard sufficiently against such a christomonistic distortion (which the late Dorothee Soelle in her American sojourn remarked often becomes, in practice, Christo-*fascism*). But subsequent Protestant experience has taught us that an exclusivist christology leads inevitably to virulent supercessionism in relation to the parental faith of Judaism and (more recently) a total incapacity for dialogue with any other religious tradition.

The stewarding of God's mysteries here must mean guarding against this christomonistic displacement of the right and necessary Protestant emphasis on Jesus as the Christ.

THE PRIORITY OF GRACE (*CONTRA* VOLUNTARISM AND DETERMINISM)

Surely the second principle of classical Protestantism must be the priority of divine grace in human salvation. In a real way, this is where the Reformation began: with the rediscovery of the Pauline conception of justification, perhaps best expressed in Ephesians 2: "By grace you have been saved, through faith; and this is not your own doing, it is the gift of God—not because of works lest any[one] should boast" (vv. 8-9 rsv). Over against the tendency of religion, especially in its institutional expressions, to base belonging and acceptability on accomplishment, adherence to ritualized ecclesiastical practices, and "works" recognized by the authorities as "good," the Reformers insisted that God is the initiator and perfecter of our redemption. Even the act of faith itself is denied such priority, for faith must not be treated as a human work. The formula of the Reformation is not "justification by faith," as it is so often misleadingly stated, but "justification by grace through faith." This is a merciful doctrine, not only in its recognition of the graciousness of God, but also in its refusal to rank human worth on the basis of achievement. Justification theology has a leveling, democratizing effect in the church just for this reason.

But as history has regularly demonstrated, this principle, too, lives with inherent temptations. On the one hand, the emphasis on the sufficiency of divine grace tempts its champions to disregard human responsibility (on which all theology of stewardship rests). That, as Dietrich Bonhoeffer demonstrated in *The Cost of Discipleship*, is the temptation from the Lutheran side of the Reformation. On the other hand, the idea of divine sovereign grace too easily transmutes into a kind of religious determinism that is ready to attribute whatever happens, including human rejection of grace, to "the fore-ordaining will of God." This is the temptation from the Calvinist side. Both of these typical temptations stem from an apparent incapacity to hold together in creative tension the affirmation of God's grace and the recognition of human freedom and responsibility. That incapacity leads directly to a third important principle of classical Protestantism:

DIALECTICAL CHARACTER OF THEOLOGY (*CONTRA* DOCTRINAL SIMPLISM)

Theology, in the classical Protestant mode, is a discipline of thought that is necessarily dialectical—ready to entertain polarities, ambiguities, paradoxes, including apparent opposites like prevenient grace and human freedom. Christian theology must do this for one very basic and unconditional reason: it deals with *living* realities—a living God, living creatures, lively and always changing relationships. The objects with which theology concerns itself are not objects but living subjects, and their interrelationships are complex and forever in flux. They do not stand still so that the theological observers can tabulate them once and for all. They do not lend themselves to definition in immutable propositional and dogmatic form. Karl Barth, who certainly cannot be accused of refraining from trying to be definitive theologically, stated both at the beginning and the ending of his long career that doing theology is like attempting to draw a picture of a bird in flight: the danger, almost the inevitability, is that one ends either with a bird permanently stuck in one position in an unchanging sky or else an unrecognizable oblong blur. I suppose one could say that "conservatism" courts the first danger and "liberalism" the second, but I am wary of using these categories at all.

This is why Protestant theology at its best has always had to be (as Barth also said) "modest"—indeed, "the most modest science"—and is constantly involved in self-criticism.[6] Theology can only point awkwardly toward the mystery of a livingness that it experiences but cannot contain. To do justice to this livingness, theology must resort to language that, especially to the modern scientific mind, seems imprecise and even inconsistent: the language of narrative, of poetry, of myth and symbol, the language of dialogue, in which every affirmation must be corrected by a qualification or counteraffirmation.

Thus, the vocation of theology in the Protestant mode has always been in a certain sense frustrating, for the human mind (including the mind of the theologian) wants finality. It wants fact, data, truth—and, by hook or by crook, it will get such, even at the expense of falsifying or ignoring the ongoingness and livingness of its subject. Moreover, in the contemporary scene, where the popular demand for finality is heightened by a pathological clamoring after *securitas* (security), this quest for certitude is vastly intensified. It is not surprising, then, that the most popular forms of Christianity on this security-obsessed continent and elsewhere today are those (most of them allegedly Protestant) that do not require continuous and profound contemplation of mystery but offer simple, immediate, and sloganized declarations of ultimate truth.

But nothing is more indicative of the plight of Protestantism in our time and place than the prevalence of just this "Protestant" simplism. The stewarding of God's mysteries (mysteries!) in such a context must mean struggling against this demand for the kind of finality that offers easy religious answers to difficult and unexamined human questions. *Life itself is not simple*, and a religion that accommodates itself to popular demand for unnuanced, undialectical, one-two-three assertions can appeal only to those who are comfortable enough physically and economically to be able to repress what they know very well to be true of life. Such persons may be very numerous in our "developed world" context; they may even be the majority. But a Protestantism that wants to win the whole world inevitably loses its own soul.

FAITH SEEKS UNDERSTANDING (*CONTRA* RATIONALISM AND IRRATIONALISM)

Classical Protestantism entertains an always-uneasy yet remarkably consistent mutuality between faith and reason. This, too, belongs to the dialectical thinking that characterizes this mode of theological thought. However, faith is not the consequence of human ratiocination. It is the human response to the revelation of the divine Presence; it is trust in the absence of clear evidence, what Paul calls "sight." I cannot bring about faith in myself or in others any more than I can bring about love. But if I find myself or another person yearning for something like faith, it is probable that the divine Instigator of faith is already at work.

However, once a person has entered into the faith relationship, the quest for understanding begins. And it is intense and relentless. *Fides quaerens intellectum*, declared Anselm of Canterbury: "faith seeks understanding." But the word *seeks* doesn't do justice to what is meant. Anselm's *quaerens* does not mean polite inquiry or having a mild interest in theology! Commenting on this phrase from Anselm's *Proslogion*, Karl Barth writes of "faith's voracious desire for understanding."[7] Faith, if it is really faith and not just spiritual froth, is *driven to* understanding—to the point that the absence of any quest for understanding must seem to this tradition to be evidence enough that faith isn't really present.

The stewarding of the Protestant tradition in this matter means maintaining a certain vigilance that the community of discipleship is not courting, on the one hand, a religious rationalism that reduces faith to a stained-glass intellectualism inaccessible to ordinary people or, on the other hand, a sentimental or apocalyptic irrationalism that settles for religious "feelings" and spiritual ecstasy. As Blaise Pascal once wrote, "If we submit everything to reason, our religion will have no mysterious and supernatural element. If we offend the principle of reason, our religion will be absurd and ridiculous."[8]

How multitudinous, where this principle is concerned, are the problems of Protestantism in our context! We could speak about the continuing allure of emotionalistic religion, ecstatic religion, spiritualism (including the spiritualism that has the name of being "new"). But before we attempt to clean up the houses of others, we should look to our own denominational houses. There we may find that the neglect of the pursuit of understanding indicates more about the demise of Protestantism than anything to be found in the realm of religious irrationalism—that and the equally damaging separation of academic theology from the ordinary discourse of congregations.[9]

It was not an incidental but a central affirmation and assumption of the Reformers that theology—the quest for understanding on the part of the faithful—is the work of the whole people of God. The Christian academy, whether of seminary or of university, exists for the sake of the church. "The true genius of Protestantism," wrote Ronald Goetz, "is to make extraordinary demands on very ordinary people."[10]

In North American Protestantism, because we have relied so heavily on our cultural form of establishment and because we have practiced great condescension toward the laity, we have made few demands of any kind upon church folk, least of all intellectual demands. It is not because the pews, or those potentially and actually present in them, are uninterested (though congregations are wonderfully adept at manifesting whatever is expected of them). Often, sitting in church during worship, I find myself irreverently thinking of John Milton's line from *Lycidas*: "The hungry sheep look up and are not fed." At a bare minimum, the stewarding of the mysteries of God must mean today and tomorrow a far greater effort on the part of clergy, "teaching elders," actually to teach. We are still—anachronistically!—pushing images of the minister as the CEO of the congregation, responsible for everything all the time, including the drumming up of enthusiasm for "stewardly" church giving, mostly a thankless task, since the whole exercise begs the question "Why?" The only answer to *that* question will be found—if it is found at all—in sermons and classes and study groups that are so seriously considered and worked upon that they can sometimes illumine the soul.

THE BIBLE (*CONTRA* BIBLICISM AND BIBLE ILLITERACY)

The *sola Scriptura* of the Reformation never meant that no other work of Christian tradition should have any importance for Protestantism, but it did and does mean that the canonical scriptures of the Older and Newer Testaments have priority. "Abandon scripture," warns Luther, "and God abandons us to the lies of human beings."[11] *In theory*, Protestantism everywhere, "core" and "wider" alike, makes the Bible central to the life of the church. But the nature of that centrality differs greatly in classical Protestantism from those forms of Protestantism that make the most noise about the Bible today. So-called biblical literalism—which is typically not a literalism of the biblical text but of certain doctrinal and moral presuppositions searched for (and, of course, regularly found) in the biblical text— is in fact antithetical to the kind of attention to the Bible that the main Reformers taught. Calvin*ism*, to be sure, has frequently been the godparent of biblical literalism, but Calvin himself, the French Reformer schooled (as were Zwingli and Philipp Melanchthon) in humanism, would certainly never approve the kind of literalism that disdains critical interpretation of the text, especially of texts that are themselves only translations of original texts.

As for the approach Martin Luther took to scripture, I suspect that it is scarcely known in most of our Protestant churches, even Lutheran ones, for it is a highly complex—indeed, wonderfully dialectical—approach and therefore goes counter to the kind of simplism to which I have already referred. On the one hand, Luther's theological method is extraordinarily informed by scripture—and concretely, not merely theoretically so. On the other hand, Luther manifests an astonishing freedom with respect to the Bible. He is not above dismissing whole sections of it. For he is a master of a *con-*

textually sensitive exegesis (Barth might have called it "pneumatic" interpretation). Such an interpretation is conscious not only of the biblical testimony itself but of the present contextual realities, the zeitgeist, the pressing human questions that are brought to the contemplation of the text by anyone who is going to it under the impact of existential need. The authority of scripture, for Luther, is its capacity to let us hear the *living* Word that always transcends without dismissing the written word. That is, through "the letter" we listen for "the spirit"—the deepest meaning—of the text for us, which surpasses yet never despises the biblical words.[12]

I have come to think that Luther's understanding of the Bible's role is the most important one for us to discern and emulate today—partly because, like so much of Luther's thought, it is so little known in the Anglo-Saxon Christian world. Yet all the Reformers have things to teach us still on this subject. Generalizing, it seems entirely clear that no major voice of the Reformation that gave Protestantism its start could condone either the biblical illiteracy of bourgeois Protestant liberalism *or* the biblicism of Christian conservatism. And that, I would say, is a very charitable way of stating the matter!

The stewardship of the mysteries of God, as these are vouchsafed to us in classical Protestantism, therefore requires enormous efforts on the part of the churches to achieve greater familiarity with the scriptures, coupled with a critical questioning of the biblicism that is rampant on this continent and is unfortunately imitated today in many parts of the developing world.

FAITH IN DIALOGUE WITH DOUBT (*CONTRA* FIDEISM OR "TRUE BELIEF")

Faith, in the Protestant mode, is not a synonym for credulity. Like all of the major biblical categories (love, hope, sin, etc.—or even nouns like *God, humankind, world,* etc.), faith is a relational concept. It is another word for trust, and its application to God (faith *in* God) is in essence not different from its application to other relationships, such as when one says one has faith in one's life companion, one's child, or one's friend. Like these relationships, faith in God is always a matter of decision and is not a fixed quality but a response that demands continuous renewal.

As decision-in-response, faith lives with its own antithesis, doubt. There are, to be sure, moments of doubt's or of faith's ascendancy in the life of discipleship, both corporately and individually understood. Yet faith is itself an ongoing dialogue with doubt, for faith is denied the kind of ultimacy that is promised as the eschatological resolution of its internal tensions—the resolution that Paul designates by the metaphor of "sight" (see, e.g., Heb 11:1). As mentioned earlier, the Spanish philosopher Miguel de Unamuno said, "A faith that does not doubt is a dead faith."[13] Although Unamuno was not a Protestant and perhaps not even a Christian, he captured in this bon mot the nature of faith as Protestants of both the Reformation and later periods have understood it: as a living trust that achieves authenticity only where it manifests consciousness of the internal and external difficulties with which *all* trust, to be trust, must struggle.

The Reformation's *sola fide* is thus not a statement about Christian acceptance of religious "truths" in the absence of any clear proof. Rather, it is a statement about the centrality of an existential trust in God that is made in the full awareness of an ongoing temptation to existential distrust: "I believe, [Lord,] help my unbelief" (Mark 9:24 rsv). "There is no faith without an intrinsic 'in spite of,'" wrote Paul Tillich.[14]

There is a tremendous need for sensitive and informed stewarding of this Protestant understanding of faith—faith that is not credulity, not "true belief," not a spiritual possession, but an act of trust that entails honesty about its antithesis. I suspect that no practical teaching of Paul Tillich has been more accessible and important to thousands of people, both laity and clergy, than his teaching concerning the ongoing dialogue of faith with doubt. This teaching has liberated many from the tyranny of a fideism that made it impossible for them to be honest about their skepticism and unbelief, and that sent countless human beings in our time out of the churches because they were persuaded by Christian faith-talk that belief had to be all or nothing, and they could not claim the "all." Apart from Luther, who was uncommonly honest about his doubts, Reformation figures did not much develop this kind of thought about the nature of faith. Many later Protestants (including Karl Barth, who once said that he wished somebody would whisper to Paul Tillich that he should not take his doubt so seriously) have done little to counter the notion that doubt is inimical to the life of faith.

But the absence of the dialectic of faith and doubt in much of the tradition does not mean that it is absent from the whole or from the scriptural foundations. Job, Ecclesiastes, many of the Psalms, Jeremiah, Lamentations, and much else in the Old Testament, including the central image of Israel as "the one who struggles with God," is precisely about this dialectic. And what of the Gospels, which from first to last tell the story of Jesus' closest associates and their ongoing vacillation between loyalty and betrayal, trust and mistrust, in relation to their "Master"? Yes—and what of Jesus himself, who in Gethsemane cries out in dereliction, feeling himself abandoned by the God in whom he trusted?

Nothing, I suspect, is more important in the stewarding of this tradition today than that pastors and teachers should take every opportunity to assure those in and around the churches that doubt and doubters are welcome in the community of faith. On this continent particularly, those who stand in the tradition of classical Protestantism cannot overestimate the manner in which religious certitude has defined for the populace as a whole the character of Christian belief and belonging. Unfortunately, this is not confined to centers of fundamentalist, biblicist, and pietist religion. It also is present in many Christian circles that have the reputation of being liberal or moderate. To admit doubt, in a society like ours that rewards winners and in churches like ours that function to squelch negation of every kind, requires a great deal of honesty and personal courage.

CONCLUSION

In any full treatment of this subject, it would, of course, be necessary to go on—and on! For example, to establish concretely what the stewardship of the Protestant tradition must entail in our particular context, it would be necessary to speak about the relational character of the biblical conception of sin. Sin is probably the most misunderstood term in the Christian vocabulary. For centuries, it has suffered the worst kind of reductionism—namely, the reduction to "sins," nasty little thoughts, words, and deeds that we can confess and be forgiven for while we carry on with being the alienated human beings whose estrangement from God, neighbor, and self *is* the sin that generates all this nastiness and much, much worse.

It would be necessary, as well, to speak about the nature of redemption—which in the classical traditions of Protestantism is for the sake of the *whole* creation, not for the selfish end of getting a few precious souls into heaven. And in that connection, it would be necessary to address the bad, misleading, and utterly inadequate theology of atonement, a soteriology that took over the entire Western world ten centuries ago and is still (as Mel Gibson's film *The Passion of the Christ* has amply demonstrated) the only atonement theology we seem to know anything about: namely, the Latin satisfaction or substitutionary doctrine of the cross. Peter Abelard rightly insisted centuries ago that this interpretation of the meaning of the cross of Christ presupposes a very questionable conception of the nature of a God whom the Bible describes not only as loving but as *being* love. Truly, the Reformation failed to do very much about that Anselmic theory, and Calvin, alas, rather gave it a boost.

But Luther didn't, and we would be well advised (if we are serious about critiquing Mel Gibson's and other bloody ideas about the meaning of the cross) to return to the little seminal study of Gustav Aulen entitled *Christus Victor*.[15] Aulen demonstrates that the earliest soteriology of the cross, which Luther particularly favored, does not present the Christ as the innocent sacrificial victim who atones for all the sins of the guilty, but as the liberator of humankind from forces of oppression greater than our strength of will—an atonement theology that not only is behind the liberation theology of our own era (though perhaps unconsciously), but speaks far more directly to our condition in this society than does Anselm's explanation of the meaning of the cross. For we are not first conscious of ourselves as guilty, but as the superfluous pawns of technocratic and economic systems and fatalized mentalities that call in question any meaning that we might once have entertained.

It would be necessary, too, to speak about the church and how it is not called to be a religious institution or even another of the world's "religions." Rather, it is to be a movement that looks for the reign of God in the midst of historical chaos and uncertainty and so becomes, now and then, a harbinger of hope in the midst of a despairing age and a floundering creation. In the area of ecclesiology, we need to pay greater attention than mainstream Protestantism has yet done to the so-called radical wing of the Reformation—the Anabaptists and others who, already in the sixteenth century and beyond, knew what it meant to live outside Christendom.

One could go on! But I have said enough to establish the point. If we are ready to renew the Protestant commitment to stewardship (and stewardship is, in fact, a vital piece of the Protestant contribution to ecumenical Christianity), then it is essential that we begin by becoming more intentionally stewards of "the mysteries of God" as these have been vouchsafed to us in the traditions of classical Protestantism. I believe, as do many others, that so far as its "core" or "classical" expression is concerned, Protestantism in the West has been pushed further and further toward the periphery of our society. In my lifetime, the old, established denominations have been replaced in the public arena by manifestations of what calls itself Protestantism but could not endorse anything like the points I have been making in this review of the commanding principles of this tradition. In fact, much of this "wider" Protestantism represents a completely different approach to theology, morality, and the nature and mission of the Christian movement.

Most of us are shocked to note the extent to which our once most-established churches have been marginalized by the events of the past four or five decades. Though for the most part they are unworthy bearers of this classical tradition, they *are* the remnants of the Protestant witness in the Western world, and they are still looked to by many rather lonely souls in the rest of the world for some kind of guidance.

We may think we are fighting a battle that has been lost already. Certainly, no battles are going to be won by creating churches that are bigger, noisier, more communications-smart, better financed,

and so on. but still lacking theological, ethical, and missiological substance. It is tempting to feel (I think every conscientious Protestant I
know is frequently tempted to feel) that we are on the way out, if we
have not already been summarily dismissed. Certainly it is folly to
imagine that we are still at the center of things in either my country
(Canada) or yours, though in the USA there is still an inordinate
temptation in that direction.

But listen! From the edges, from the sidelines, it is possible for
the once-mainline church to exercise a *prophetic* ministry, a *public*
witness that it could not easily bring off and seldom did bring off
when it was still an unquestioned part of the Establishment. Nothing has been more encouraging to me and other Canadians and Europeans of late than the manner in which important segments of
all of the once-established Protestant churches of the United States,
including the National Council of Churches, said no to the unfortunate war against Iraq, for which we are all reaping the whirlwind
that its instigators sowed. I doubt the churches could have done that
a century ago. Even with regard to Vietnam, many of them were still
ambiguous enough in their loyalties to hold back from forthright
protest.

What is needed now, surely, is a theological rigor and discipline
that can give the necessary ideational and spiritual backing to this
newfound moral courage of American Protestantism to go against
the grain of institutions and classes that in the past have been its chief
supporters. All is not lost with the Protestant (the *Protest*-ant) mainstream. In fact, it could be only now undergoing preparation for the
ministry that has been its potential all along. Its sidelining *could* be
the very sociological condition that is preparing it for a prophetic
ministry—indeed, for the stewarding of history. But although that
is the very purpose and rationale for stewarding "the mysteries of
God" in their Protestant form, it is yet another topic.

CHAPTER FOUR

Words

For as the rain and the snow come down from heaven,
    and return not thither but water the earth,
making it bring forth and sprout,
    giving seed to the sower and bread to the eater,
so shall my word be that goes forth from my mouth;
    it shall not return to me empty,
but it shall accomplish that which I purpose,
    and prosper in the thing for which I sent it.

                              —Isaiah 55:10-11 RSV

One of Germany's most honored and provocative writers, Günter Grass, wrote a story in 1979 that is not well known in the English-speaking literary world, though it has been translated into English as well as other languages. It is called *Das Treffen in Telgte* (The Meeting in Telgte).[1] It is a story about words and the people whose vocation is to be wordsmiths. Theologians too are such people.

Those who know the works of Günter Grass will realize that this story, like his others, has a strong didactic—well, a frankly political—intent. Grass, like many other poets of our age, knows himself to be living in an age when words have become cheap—an age, however, when the *right* words are needed more than ever.

In "The Meeting in Telgte," Grass revisits with poetic license one of the most critical periods in European (especially German) history: the first part of the seventeenth century. During this era, there occurred what was later called the Thirty Years War. The armies of most of the western European nations ranged back and forth over the scorched landscape for three decades. Germany, then comprising numerous little kingdoms, was a virtual battle-field. The slaughter was horrendous and wholly capricious. By 1642 Germany was exhausted, its population decimated. Peace negotiations between the nations had begun in 1640, but it was not until 1648 that the famous Peace of Westphalia was signed in the city hall of Münster, a beautiful north German city that I regard as my European home.

This is the setting for Günter Grass's novel. Telgte is a little town, a Catholic pilgrimage town, very near Münster and Osnabrück, the two cities where all the diplomats and military leaders had gathered to see whether life could go on after all those years of devastation. To little Telgte Grass summons, in imagination, all the famous poets and writers of the age. While the great politicians are working out the terms of the Peace of Westphalia, the poets have been brought together to work out their own statement. Can art rise above the clamor of the nations and princedoms? Can truth transcend the compromises and mutual suspicions and power plays of the movers and shakers of history? Can words be found that might give despairing humanity a little courage to go on, as Elie Wiesel says, to "begin again"?

At first, the gathering of the poets is full of promise. Buchner, Dach, Greflinger, von Grimmelhausen, and the others enthrall one another with their brilliant essays, poems, and stories. Even Paul Gerhard, author of the famous Passion hymn "O Sacred Head, Now Wounded," is there. The hopes of this gathering of the age's great wordsmiths are running high. They are confident they will be able to produce a common statement that will move their society to new levels of hope and human endeavor.

After days and weeks of work, however, the poets find that they are themselves caught up in the complications, half-truths, and subterfuge of the general human condition. One fine morning, their whole enterprise comes to a shattering halt when the writers are brought to the realization that the marvelous banquet they had enjoyed the night before—an unheard-of, bounteous feast at a time of dreadful, universal want—had been procured by one of their own number, a scoundrel who had lied, plundered, and killed to acquire the wherewithal for their merrymaking.

Then the poets sink into deep despair—and into silence. *They* would not be able to speak from beyond the crisis. They were simply part of it. Their document, they knew, "would not be a protest, but only a statement of the usual helplessness. No need to trumpet that. That's not what they had met for. So why *were* they sitting there?"

At this moment of bleak despondency, someone arises—the guest of honor. Not, by the way, a poet. Not a writer. Rather, a musician: the famous court musician of the age, Heinrich Schütz. Why had they come? Why were they sitting there? "For the sake," said Schütz, "of the written words, which poets alone had the power to write in accordance with the dictates of art. And also to wrest from the helplessness—he knew it well—a faint 'and yet.'"

And yet . . . The German word is *dennoch*. To "wrest from helplessness" a feeble yet sober *nevertheless*.

After this, the poets find themselves enabled, gradually, hesitantly, to take up the task once more—"speaking," as Grass puts it—"speaking into the . . . erupting silence."

∽

The story speaks for itself, but I shall allow myself a brief commentary. Why are *we* here at Trinity Lutheran Seminary? This too is a gathering of those who would find words—this seminary, and indeed the whole movement, the Christian church, that it is called to serve. Our enterprise stands or falls on our capacity, corporately and individually, to comprehend and articulate through language the profound meaning that we sense dimly on the edges of our consciousness and our small attempts at scholarship. We know that great deeds are being done and great decisions made in the towers of the nearby city, in the mansions of our well-to-do neighborhoods, in the cities and universities and corporations of our advanced technological civilization. By comparison, we feel even at the best of times that our enterprise is rather peripheral, perhaps even redundant. There are moments when we suspect that our quest—the quest for "the right words"—matters not at all in the scheme of things.

Words have become so cheap, so easy. The world is full of them, and most of them are empty, predictable, and self-promotional. Imagine the chaos to which the universe is daily subjected by the welter of words rising up from planet Earth! Words calculated to impress, to sell, to persuade. Words meant from the start not to reveal but to hide the truth. Words uttered for no other purpose than to fill the blank places in our lives. How worthless must the words of the wordy, consumer societies of the possessing peoples of this world seem to those great wordsmiths of our civilization whom we honor with our lips: to Shakespeare, Milton, Plato, Cervantes, Balzac, and the others.

And then, too, like the poets of Telgte, we are brought now and then to know how much we ourselves are a part of all the chaos and equivocation and self-interest of the world. We have our ideals. We want to transcend the superficiality of the slick world of the advertisers. Yet we wear the products they tell us are chic, "cool," and we drive their cars and delight in their technologies. Where would we be without our laptops? We even measure our own success, the success of wordsmiths, by their same standards: do our words sell, are they marketable, do they impress, can they enhance our résumés and make for eloquent introductions on public occasions? We have come here in hope, as the poets came to their little pilgrimage town, but how hard it is to nurture these hopes when the quest for knowledge is daily sacrificed to the scurry for "information" and when standing seems infinitely more important than understanding.

So, often enough, we too find ourselves on the edge of debilitating despondency. We all too frequently become conscious of "the erupting silence" and our apparent helplessness in the face of it.

And my only intention, standing here at this lectern, just a few inches above the world's derisive contradiction, is to reiterate—in somewhat altered language—the message of Günter Grass's Heinrich Schütz—especially that little word *dennoch*: "And yet!" Precisely as those who know the silence and the helplessness—indeed, *only* as those who know this—we may also hear from time to time the permission that is given us to "speak into the erupting silence."

This permission emanates from the very core of the Word that has summoned us to our "Telgte." For that Word is nothing more nor less than God's own great nevertheless to a creation spoiled and desolate. That is why we have to become conscious again and again of the helplessness and the silence. Without these, we are prone to take it all for granted—as if it were entirely natural, as if words could easily be found and fashioned to accomplish the task at hand. We must undergo the humiliation and the silence again and again if we are to hear with gratitude and joy God's Word, living and impossible to possess, to which our words can only faintly bear witness.

Yet they can do that! Only God's Word, foolishness and *skandalon* though it seems to the great and wise ones of the world, can give us the courage to "begin again." Only God's Word does not return to its Speaker void. Yet our words, hesitant and awkward though they be, being taken up by that eternal Speaker—called *Deus loquens* by Luther—will bring forth hearing and faith in some.

Let us have courage, therefore, as God's poets. Let us trust that our words, even ours, will accomplish what they are meant to accomplish—which may not, of course, include the fate of being stirring oratory, world-illuminating wisdom, or the best-selling books of theology that we, being sinful, desire for them.

Amen.

CHAPTER FIVE

De Profundis:

On Going "Right Deep Down into Life"

The late English humorist P. G. Wodehouse had the following to say about the writing of novels: "I believe there are two ways of writing novels. One is mine, making a sort of musical comedy without music and ignoring real life altogether; the other is going right deep down into life and not caring a damn."[1]

Such a generalization could, with a little adjustment, be applied to the writing of theology. Rather too much religious literature over the centuries falls under the first of Wodehouse's types: not necessarily "musical comedy without music" (since most of it is singularly lacking in humor) but definitely "ignoring real life altogether."

In fact, ignoring real life is a particular temptation for religious authors, as it is for theorists in many other fields of human endeavor—political and economic theory, for example. It is possible—easily possible and perhaps even usual—for the religious to live entirely within the tent of their faith tradition and restrict their discourse to like-minded members of their own spiritual persuasion. This has always been a temptation for the religious, but it may be a particular temptation in our time—above all, perhaps, for Christians in the once monolithically Christian West. As Christianity finds itself pushed out of the limelight as the favored cultus of the official culture in Western societies; as it notices that it must now share that stage with many other players, both religious and secular; and as it becomes conscious of being confronted by ontological and moral questions that are both unprecedented and disconcerting, many of its most dogmatic practitioners tend to withdraw into their own spiritual fortresses and write books for their own kind. Such Christianity no longer feels obliged to go out into the marketplace to find out what is happening there, for it believes that its doctrine has already accounted for anything and everything that could possibly occur in the world, most of it under the nomenclature "sin." Its communication with its worldly context will be chiefly one-way. Pronouncements will be made, moral judgments issued, and human questions "answered."

That the answers address questions nobody outside the religious community is currently asking is not a concern for the cloistered religious. Indeed, part of the allure of such religion is precisely that it cunningly displaces contemporary anxieties by focusing upon the spiritual preoccupations and quests of yesteryear. It is thus quite possible to live entirely beneath the canopy of religious convention, and to do so very successfully, as the current church statistics of our continent corroborate. Apparently it is exactly in avoiding real life with its ongoing complexity and bewilderment, and doing so in a showy and self-assured manner, that religion achieves its greatest popularity.

The other approach to the writing of novels—and, I would say, of theology—is, in Wodehouse's characteristically breezy terms, "going right deep down into life and not caring a damn." With admirable self-knowledge, the great humorist does not claim that approach for his own, yet implicitly he recognizes that this approach must be risked by all authors who want to write about life as it is actually lived.

I doubt that anyone ever actually chooses such an approach. I'm sure William Shakespeare frequently wished he could have stuck to the entertaining farces that were the diversions sought out by the masses of his era, rather than plunging into something as "deep down" as *King Lear* or *The Winter's Tale* or *The Tempest*. Leo Tolstoy and Fyodor Dostoyevsky would both have had much happier lives had they been able to pursue tales of courtly love and political intrigue among the decadent aristocracy of czarist Russia instead of the devastating themes of faith and doubt, hope and despair, love and death that permeate their great literary creations. Who would choose to chronicle the career of a Raskolnikov or an Anna Karenina and be led by such lives as these to contemplate in the most concrete form the pathos and promise, the longing and tragedy of human existence?

It is not otherwise in theology. Only someone as driven by events or by the divine Spirit as was Jeremiah would dare to pursue a faith that would lead him into exile and make him wish (in chapter 20) that he had never been born. Only a soul that had been turned right around, as was Saul of Tarsus, would spend his life contemplating the meaning of the cross of Golgotha, when such contemplation, seriously undertaken, must clearly mean his own incorporation into the suffering endured there. Only a life denied the spiritual safety of the monastery and forced to trust the God it could not capture nor even understand would risk—as Martin Luther had to—exposure to the terrible questions and contradictions that confronted European humanity with the breakdown of the medieval synthesis.

Delving "right deep down into life," as all authentic Judeo-Christian theology must do, occurs only in those who feel a strong sense of obligation. It is a matter of *vocation*. To the extent that one does it at all, this calling incorporates an awareness (in Paul's language) of a certain inexorable *necessitas*: "Necessity is laid upon me; yea, woe is unto me, if I preach not the gospel" (1 Cor 9:16 KJV). The word for necessity in Greek is *anangke*—literally, destiny, even fate. Just as Shakespeare, Tolstoy, and Dostoyevsky were somehow destined to write the novels they wrote, so Jeremiah, Paul, and Luther went "right deep down into life" as persons who knew they had no other choice. To picture them as writers of musical comedies or of lighthearted or "edifying" religious tracts ("How to Find God," "How to Pray Effectively," "Achieving Peace of Mind") is inconceivable. They were compelled by their immersion in the great crises of their times and by the Spirit of God that still broods over those deep waters to go where ordinary human curiosity would never have taken them, where ordinary human courage would not suffice. They all understood that caveat that Jesus whispers to the apostle Peter at the end of John's Gospel: "When thou wast young, thou girdest thyself, and walkedst whither thou wouldest: but when thou shalt be old, thou shalt stretch forth thy hands, and another shall gird thee, and carry thee *whither thou wouldest not*" (21:18 KJV; italics added).

The other side of this sense of destiny, this drivenness, however, is a wonderful freedom. The two polarities, destiny and freedom, here again inform and qualify one another, as they always do when they are profoundly conceived. The one who feels driven in the service of the gospel to delve deeply into the unknown reality of today and tomorrow is simultaneously sustained by the belief that the powers by which he is carried "whither he would not go" are also powers that are able to illumine the dark places into which he is being taken.

This is what P. G. Wodehouse is getting at when he says that the second type of novelist (which he himself is not) goes "right deep down into life and [*doesn't care*] a *damn*." That is Wodehouse's irreverent but rather graphic way of speaking about the freedom that the novelist feels with respect to what others may think, what the critics may write, what the buying public will make of his or her story, or even what the novelist, as a person of pride and ambition, would like to achieve. Such a writer has been pulled by creative forces greater than him- or herself into realms of human mystery that cannot be accounted for easily or without personal anguish. So everything else—the opinion of the literary guild, the sniping of the chattering classes, the lure of the best-seller lists, the articles in *Who's Who*, the applause of the public, and even the author's own natural human desire for recognition, fame, and economic success—all that is pushed aside by the new freedom that the author senses, freedom to follow where his or her Muse leads, come what may.

It is surely this paradox of destiny and freedom, of drivenness and self-forgetfulness that we encounter in the works of all the great theologians. Consider Augustine, the classics scholar and rhetorician. If he had to be a Christian, he would rather have been a monk, yet driven by the divine Spirit into the dark public arena of his epoch, that tumultuous age of the fall of Rome, he freely wrote of his tragic epoch and of what God was doing in it. And there is Thomas Aquinas, the monk, at heart the mystic but destined by his calling to think the faith anew in a historical moment when the nature of thinking itself—reasoning—was being redefined. How boldly in his *Summae* he plunges into every corner of human life and knowledge, "not caring a damn" (might we not say?) how his work will be received, just doing what he must do. Søren Kierkegaard, the romantic, sensitive, earnest young Dane in love with Regina, wanted so much to be "normal" but was compelled by forces greater than himself to unmask the hypocrisies of Christendom and the sickness unto death of mid-nineteenth-century European humanity. With what elegant freedom he does it, in what unforgettable prose! And Paul Tillich, the thinker, the philosopher, the compulsive, was seemingly marked for fame in his own land, but at forty-seven years of age was driven from his *Heimat* by Germany's terrible internal contradictions and had to work out his own salvation in fear and trembling in a very foreign land. Yet with what liberty and clarity he details the ending of modernity and the rebirth of "New Being" out of its ashes.

The writing of theology (and that includes every sincere and disciplined preacher) entails this kind of exposure to the heights and depths, the hopes and despairs, the beauties and terrors of life as it is lived in the *hic et nunc*. It is no safe profession! Like Abraham, the theologian has to go out without knowing where he or she is going. One has to enter the unknown land, the terra incognita, of the present and impending future and to confront, as though one had no ready-made religious responses, the searing dilemmas of today and tomorrow. The theologian, the preacher, is not sheltered from that unknown by the certitudes of doctrinal tradition. Rather, these certitudes are subjected to high criticism—and not only or chiefly to the skepticism and cynicism of human courts, but to the burning winds of the divine Spirit, who will have us learn discipleship through loss of all easy, inherited preconceptions. Confidence we may now and then feel; certitude never. That we are in touch with Truth we may sense, now and then, here and there; that we *possess* Truth, never.

Like most human beings (novelists, theologians, whomsoever), I have often wished that I could be, à la P. G. Wodehouse or Stephen Leacock, a writer of lighthearted and entertaining pieces, a preacher of happiness, peace of mind, and spiritual fulfillment—or at least of timely topics that would achieve high visibility and the usual rewards. But I have felt compelled by something beyond my personal inclinations to contemplate, in the midst of an age that has nearly lost the meaning of contemplation, a tradition that leads toward light only those whom it first conducts into deep darkness, and not just once, but again and again.

Yet far from producing in me a sense of the futility of all human endeavor (futility does not write books!), this vocation to delve "right deep down into life" without counting the cost has given me something like a sense of adventure—a kind of curious and absorbing expectancy that I know I should not otherwise have experienced. For the message at the core of our stumbling theological and preacherly attempts to comprehend and articulate it is just what Kierkegaard claimed when he wrote of it: "The gospel is not melancholy; it is 'glad tidings'—for the melancholy. For the frivolous it is of course not so, for it wishes to make them serious."[2]

As that line of "the melancholy Dane" typically if subtly shows, however, readers of the works of those who delve "right deep down into life" must also reckon with the prospect that they shall have to spend a good deal of time in the depths and darkness if they are to attain whatever intimations of the heights and the light may present themselves in these outpourings. Many readers of Christian literature, I have found, wish only to be uplifted—and with the least possible expenditure of either psychic or intellectual effort on their part. The famous "pursuit of happiness" is perhaps nowhere more frantically active than in the search for religious and parareligious literature that banishes melancholy by presenting life as "a sort of musical comedy without music." One is reminded of Franz Kafka's line, "Books that make everybody happy we could write ourselves, if forced to do so!"[3]

The book that the Academy of Parish Clergy has honored with a deeply moving award[4] is not a book calculated to make everybody *happy*. I can only hope that it will make some who read it *joyful*, as only those can be who ponder again the joyous mystery—the gospel—of a God who enters into complete solidarity with our difficult, perhaps even impossible kind of creaturehood, joyful as souls called out of the depths by a Spirit still at work "giving life to the dead and bringing something out of nothing" (Rom 4:17 RSV).

Notes

PREFACE

1. Paolo Coelho, *The Alchemist*, trans. Alan R. Clarke (San Francisco: HarperCollins, 1993), ix–x.

INTRODUCTION

1. According to Roland Bainton, Luther's associate Justus Jonas remarked that it was Luther's new conception of vocation "which emptied the cloisters." Bainton, *Here I Stand: A Life of Martin Luther* (New York: New American Library, 1950), 156.

2. No less a "professional" theologian than Karl Barth insists that the term *theologian* is not to be reserved for professors of theology or ministers, but "for every Christian who is mindful of the theological task entrusted to the whole Christian congregation." Barth, *The Humanity of God* (Richmond: John Knox Press, 1960), 89.

3. The Church of the Crossroads in Honolulu, Hawaii.

4. For further reading on the subject of this section—and indeed this introduction as a whole—see John B. Cobb Jr., *Becoming a Thinking Christian: If We Want Church Renewal We Will Have to Renew Thinking in the Church* (Nashville: Abingdon, 1993).

5. On this subject, see Sallie McFague, *Life Abundant: Rethinking Theology and Economy for a Planet in Peril* (Minneapolis: Fortress Press, 2001), "A Brief Credo: A Religious Autobiography," 3ff.

6. "Statistics," *The Encyclopedia of Protestantism* 4, ed. Hans J. Hillerbrand (New York: Routledge, 2004), 1809–16.

7. In the wake of the recent (2004) presidential election in the United States, many commentators have noted that, while Mr. Bush could count on the support of a "Christian Right," the mainline or "old-line" churches seemed to have given very little leadership, even though large numbers (if not the majority) of their clergy and people were critical of the religious and moral conservatism of the Republican Party.

8. Jürgen Moltmann, *A Passion for God's Reign*, ed. Miroslav Volf (Grand Rapids: Eerdmans, 1998), 2.

CHAPTER ONE: ON BEING A CHRISTIAN THEOLOGIAN

This chapter originally was an address delivered at St. John's College, College-ville, Minnesota, April 20, 2002, at an occasion honoring the work of Father Kilian McDonnell on his eightieth birthday. Kilian McDonnell was founder of the Institute for Ecumenical and Cultural Research. The address was subsequently published in Theology Today *59(3): 421–27.*

1. Rolf Joachim Erler and Reiner Marquard, *A Karl Barth Reader* (Grand Rapids: Eerdmans, 1986), 112.

2. WA 5.163.28.

3. Quoted by James Carroll as the epigraph to his important work *Constantine's Sword: The Church and the Jews, a History* (Boston: Houghton Mifflin, 2001).

CHAPTER TWO: A THEOLOGIAN'S JOURNEY

This chapter gathers together three addresses prepared in response to an invitation from the Rt. Rev. Margaret Payne, Lutheran bishop of New England, who some four or five years ago asked me to address her clergy on this subject— a request unique in my experience on the lecture circuit. Bishop Payne even suggested the three subtitles, which I have retained here as the major subheads. Later, I presented a somewhat revised version of the lectures for the Church of the Crossroads in Honolulu, where I was theologian in residence for several weeks in 2003. The present version is considerably revised and (especially in the case of the second talk) enlarged. I have wished, however, to keep the speaking style of the talks, which were not intended for academic audiences but for laity, clergy, students, and others interested in the life of the church through the twentieth and into the twenty-first centuries.

1. Plato, *Apology: The Works of Plato,* ed. Irwin Edman (New York: Modern Library, 1928), 84.

2. My great-great-great-great-great-grandfather was Joseph Brant, chief of the Mohawk Nation, who was rewarded by the British Crown for his part in resisting the American Revolution by being given a large tract of land along the Grand River. The city of Brantford, in southwestern Ontario, is named after him, and he figures rather largely in the history of Canada. It tells another side of this history, however, that I did not know of this "Indian connection" until well into my adult life—when it had become all right to acknowledge such associations!

3. See Karl Barth, "The Strange, New World within the Bible," in *The Word of God and the Word of Man*, trans. Douglas Horton (New York: Harper & Row, 1957), 28ff. This 1916 essay by Barth, who was still a pastor and only just beginning to be known beyond the confines of his Swiss canton, remains for me one of the most important statements I have ever read on the nature of the Bible. It ought to be made compulsory reading for every candidate for ministry in our Bible-belted North American continent. In 1953, my first year at Union Seminary, it *was* required reading—and in an institution that can hardly be accused of being "Barthian," let alone a notorious outpost of the Bible Belt.

4. I have written a little about my childhood and adolescent experience of the church in two publications, *The Future of the Church: Where Are We Headed?* (Toronto: United Church of Canada Publishing House, 1989), and *Why Christian? For Those on the Edge of Faith* (Minneapolis: Fortress Press, 1998). My brother Keith, a retired mathematician and self-described agnostic, feels that I have been far too hard on the village church of our childhood. "They did what they could," he told me, thus demonstrating once again how the skeptical are often more tolerant than the reputedly faithful. He is probably right. I came to have expectations of the church that are likely far too demanding. It's a professional handicap: the Christian faith, to those who get close to it, is such an engrossing account of existence that one hates to see it reduced to Sunday school religion. Also, such reductions are never quite as innocent as they can seem to less questioning spirits.

5. The three deserve to be named. The Rev. Dr. Ray McLeary was an Irish-Canadian who was for years minister of a remarkable church of my denomination situated on Queen Street East in Toronto, one of the poorest sections of that metropolis. He had been a famous and beloved chaplain during World War II and was practically a living saint in the eyes of

his congregation (WoodGreen United Church) after he returned to them when the war ended. To walk down Queen Street with Ray McLeary was an unforgettable experience; everyone he met, every kid, every bum, every ex-con knew him as a friend—and he knew them, too—*by name*. He was the one who made it possible for me to go to Toronto to study music at the Royal Conservatory in 1948.

The Rev. Robert W. Miller, who had studied at Union Seminary and Emmanuel College in Toronto and later became Study Secretary of the Student Christian Movement of Canada, was on his way to New College in Edinburgh to take up the traveling fellowship of Emmanuel when I first met him in 1948. His letters to me from Edinburgh, Basel (where he studied with Barth), and Bad Boll, Germany, as well as his unique charisma as a human being, inspired in me a new and evocative conception of what it meant to be Christian in our time.

The Rev. Arthur E. Young, who became McLeary's associate at WoodGreen, was the most literate and theologically sophisticated preacher I had ever met. His sermons made me realize that Christian ministry and theology, not music, were my true vocation.

6. See Roland Bainton's translation of it in Bainton, *The Martin Luther Christmas Book* (Philadelphia: Westminster, 1948), 19–21, 37–40.

7. As I argued in a recent article for *The Lutheran*, of all the principal Reformers of the fifteenth and sixteenth centuries, Luther is the least known—especially in Anglo-Saxon circles. Indeed, reviews of the recent film *Martin Luther*, directed by Eric Till and starring Joseph Fiennes, have noted that a very high percentage of U.S. Americans (some said up to 85 percent) do not know who the sixteenth-century Martin Luther was and confuse the name with that of Martin Luther King Jr.

Even within the churches, where Luther's name is certainly known, there is a great deal of uncertainty about what he stood for. In Anglo-Christian circles, we tend to lump him together with John Calvin, Huldrych Zwingli, John Knox, and later reformers like John Wesley. But, as I shall argue in the second address, his theology is by no means easily compatible with any of these, and it is also rather notoriously "un-American" in its refusal to deal in the kind of "positive thinking" that wants no truck with the negative. See "The Theology of the Cross for Our Day," *The Lutheran* (March 2004): pp. 12ff. See also the newly published biography by Martin E. Marty, *Martin Luther* (New York: Penguin, 2004).

8. Douglas John Hall, *Remembered Voices: Reclaiming the Legacy of "Neo-Orthodoxy"* (Louisville: Westminster John Knox, 1998).

9. The lectures were later published as *Evangelical Theology: An Introduction*, trans. Grover Foley (New York: Holt, Rinehart and Winston, 1963). Following Barth's American visit, Grover Foley wrote me a lengthy letter in which he detailed many of Barth's experiences in "the land of the free," some of them not printable at the time (such as Barth's awareness that the dean of the Chicago faculty sponsoring his visit had fallen fast asleep during his lecture). Particularly illuminating were the two symposia involving a whole bevy of luminaries—Jaroslav Pelikan (panel moderator), the conservative scholar Edward Carnell from Fuller Seminary, Hans Frei of Yale, Jakob Petuchowski of Hebrew Union College, Bernard Cook, S.J., of Marquette University, Schubert Ogden of Southern Methodist University, and William Stringfellow, lawyer in New York. It was clear that Barth found Stringfellow the most compatible—and later said so. The great man winced when moderator Pelikan, thanking him at the end of the second evening, drew rather unaccountably on the prologue of John's Gospel and applied to Barth (!) the words John applies to *the Christ*, "And from his fullness have we all received, grace upon grace" (1:16 RSV).

For me, the most moving moment of the weeklong event in the Rockefeller Chapel of the University of Chicago was Barth's closing statement, which he offered in spontaneous, broken, but entirely understandable English:

> If I myself were an American citizen and a Christian and a theologian, then I would try to elaborate a theology of freedom—a theology of freedom from, let us say, an inferiority complex over against good old Europe from whence you all came, or your father. You do not need to have such an inferiority complex. That is what I have learned these weeks. You may also have freedom from a superiority complex, let us say, over against Asia and Africa. That's a complex without reason. Then I may add—your theology should also be marked by freedom from fear of communism, Russia, inevitable nuclear warfare and generally speaking, from all the aforementioned principalities and powers. Freedom for which you would stand would be the freedom for—I like to say a single word—humanity. Being an American theologian, I would then look at the Statue of Liberty in the New York Harbor. I have not seen that lady, except in pictures. Next week I shall see her in person. That lady needs a little or, perhaps, a good bit of demythologization. Nevertheless, maybe she can also be seen and interpreted and understood as a symbol of a true theology, not

of liberty, but of freedom. Well, it would be necessarily, a theology of freedom. Of that freedom to which the Son frees us, and which as His gift, is the one real human freedom.

My last question for this evening is this: Will such a specific American theology one day arise? I hope so.

The entire discussion of the two evenings was transcribed in *Criterion* (Divinity School of the University of Chicago) 2(1) (winter 1963). This quotation is found on p. 24 of that document.

10. It was, of course, the first, smaller edition of the book, published by the SCM Press of London in 1948, translated by R. H. Fuller with a foreword by Bonhoeffer's English friend George Bell, Bishop of Chichester, and a memoir of Bonhoeffer by his Jewish brother-in-law, G. Leibholz.

11. Dietrich Bonhoeffer, *Letters and Papers from Prison*, enlarged ed., ed. Eberhard Bethge (Munich: Chr. Kaiser Verlag, 1970; London: SCM, 1971).

12. I do not think that this is an exaggeration. In addition to all the works that were published during his lifetime, Barth left an immense treasure of unpublished manuscripts. Just a few years after Barth's death in 1968, I met one of his literary executors, his colleague Max Geiger, who told me, "Even his garage is filled with boxes of writings. We hardly know where to begin!"

13. I never referred to myself as a Barthian, even though, in my postgraduate years at Union Seminary, I used to be pointed out as the only Barthian in captivity there. But I was certainly deeply impressed by his writings and still quote him frequently. However, as I explained in chapter 1, there came a time in my life when I felt I had to distance myself from Barth in order to become more thoroughly grounded in my own historical and cultural context.

14. It has very little, if anything, in common with what today is being called "radical orthodoxy," even though some of the representatives of that phenomenon like to claim Barth as one of their sort. See my article "Neo-Orthodoxy" in *The Encyclopedia of Protestantism* 3, ed. Hans J. Hillerbrand (New York: Routledge, 2004), 1378–82.

15. This major work of Tillich was published over a period of more than twelve years and, of course, written over a much longer period. Volume 1 appeared in 1951, just prior to my sojourn at Union Seminary, volume 2 came out in 1957 when I was completing my STM, and volume 3 was published in 1963, the year I received my doctorate in

theology from Union Seminary. All are published by the University of Chicago Press.

Tillich retired from Union Seminary just as I was completing my master of divinity degree. When he returned (from Harvard) two years later to deliver a series of prestigious lectures over a period of several weeks, John Bennett, for whom I was teaching assistant and who regarded me as Tillich's most consistent critic among the graduate students (which may have been true at that point), asked me to prepare in advance questions to put to Tillich immediately after each lecture. Dr. Bennett with some justification feared that leaving the question period completely open to the large audience would be disastrous, so he asked me to read the relevant sections in the *Systematics* and prepare carefully considered questions, copies of which Tillich would have in advance.

It was a scary adventure for a graduate student! I labored over those questions as I've labored over little else. Imagine my chagrin, then, when with nearly every one of the questions (particularly the more critical ones), the great theologian would begin, "Now, what does this question really mean?" Very soon it would be *his* question and mine no longer. It is a useful technique, and I have frequently drawn upon it in later life.

16. See the introduction to this book.

17. The United Church of Canada was the first "united" church in North America, being a union of all the Methodists, all the Congregationalists, and two-thirds of the Presbyterian Church in 1925. It is the largest Protestant church in Canada and, until recently, the most culturally "established" of all. It has always had a strong social consciousness and program, and many U.S. Americans are still surprised to learn that the socialist political alternative that has been so important in Canadian history and experience was the product, in large measure, of the kind of "social gospel" espoused by clergy of the United Church, as well as some Baptist and other clergy. John Coleman Bennett used to say how exemplary he found it that the United Church of Canada combined "evangelism" and "social service" in one department. During the past three or four decades, the United Church has (I would say) overcome its tendency to reflect the dominant culture too closely and has adopted a more prophetically critical stance on both theological and ethical issues. It is perceived today as "radical" in a manner not the case in my childhood and youth.

18. Since I was obliged to lecture on philosophy of religion, ethics, and homiletics in addition to my own field of systematic theology, my regimen of careful preparation amounted to the equivalent of writing at

least one term paper a day. I shall not forget the morning when, after an all-night session of frenzied research and writing, I had to announce to my class of fifteen or twenty young men (no women yet) that I had nothing to offer them that morning. I simply could not be satisfied with the lecture I had prepared. I told them they could go and read. They stared at me in shocked disbelief. I expect that is the best-remembered "lecture" of my tenure at St. Andrew's. At a time when professors could easily get away with winging it, I couldn't bring myself to bluff. I had too high a conception of what a lecture should be. I still have—to the point of being dissatisfied with many of the lectures I myself offer.

19. J. A. T. Robinson, *Honest to God* (London: SCM, 1963).

20. Louisville: Westminster John Knox, 2002. Archbishop Williams was asked to write about the reception of the original publication in Great Britain, and I was asked to do the same for North America. When I met Bishop Robinson some two years before his death, I was deeply impressed by his genuine modesty and the authenticity of his faith. I remember in particular one question he put to us at that time: "Was Jesus all the God of God there is?" I have not forgotten the wording of that question, for it leaves one to ponder the nature of Christian theism and, especially in these days, the manner in which conceptions of God in other faiths can contribute positively to a Christian theism that has not substituted Christomonism for Christocentrism.

21. I am in great sympathy with Elizabeth Sifton's lament, in her recent reflections on the life and work of her father, Reinhold Niebuhr, and his generation, for the loss of concern for the whole—the whole tradition, the whole human condition, the whole church—that characterized the work of these Christian leaders, as well as her view that "single-issue groups" are problematic. I am perhaps less critical of the identity- and cause-based theologies than she, for I think those voices needed to be incorporated into the dialogue of the church. But too often, especially in the more liberal and moderate ecclesiastical communities, they tended to *become* the voice of the church. This has detracted considerably from the "catholicity" that is necessary to a faith community that must make room for more than one kind of human experience and need under its umbrella. See Sifton, *The Serenity Prayer: Faith and Politics in Times of Peace and War* (New York: W. W. Norton, 2003).

22. Quoted by Gordon Rupp, *Luther's Progress to the Diet of Worms* (New York: Harper, 1964), 38.

23. Douglas John Hall, *Lighten Our Darkness: Towards an Indigenous Theology of the Cross* (Philadelphia: Westminster, 1976).

24. I have always been glad that my first book was published (in 1972) by the World Student Christian Federation, with no solicitation on my part. Its publication was proposed, I have heard, by W. A. Visser t'Hooft, the great general secretary of the World Council of Churches, whom I met and corresponded with later, and who was one of those who most encouraged my initial endeavors as a writer of theology. The Student Christian Movement of Canada, part of the international network represented by the WSCF, was certainly for both me and my wife, Rhoda Palfrey, the most important ecumenical and theological influence through our undergraduate years and—especially in her case—beyond. I fully agree with Jürgen Moltmann when he says that the ecumenical movement is probably the greatest achievement of Christianity in the twentieth century. The SCM was the organization, in Britain, Europe, Canada, and elsewhere, that nurtured most of those who later became founders and leaders of the World Council of Churches and other ecumenical bodies.

25. Douglas John Hall, *Lighten Our Darkness: Towards an Indigenous Theology of the Cross*, rev. ed., rev. and with a foreword by David J. Monge (Lima, Ohio: Academic Renewal Press, 2001).

26. I do not mean this in a merely formal or sentimental way. Rhoda Catherine Palfrey, whom I married in 1960 while she was pursuing an MA in the history of thought at Columbia University and Union Seminary, would have had a brilliant academic career in philosophy, history, literature, or theology (she had background in all these) had she not ventured into the unknown with me at age thirty. In 1950, she had gone to Japan to teach in a church-based girls' school for three years after her graduation from Mount Allison University in the Canadian Maritimes, her homeland. She was national mission secretary with the Canadian Student Christian Movement for three years (1953–56) and a university representative of the SCM for two more. She has taught in a university faculty of education and engaged in church work at the international, national, and local levels. She reads more widely than I have ever done and is the best built-in research assistant imaginable. Our marriage of more than forty years has been a continuous seminar on many subjects—often heatedly pursued! She is present in all my books and articles and speeches. Unlike the Moltmanns, the Bob Browns, and others, we have never been able to write things together, and she regrets sometimes how haphazard and sporadic our discourse has to be, given family responsibilities and my itinerant lifestyle. But she is the

reason why I have been able to think, write, and engage in a public career, etc., etc., etc.

27. George P. Grant is unfortunately not as well known in the United States as in Canada. He is a member of a patrician academic family; his grandfather was president of Queen's University, his father headmaster of Upper Canada College. George wrote relatively few books, but they were brilliant and decisive for many of us in Canada. His most popular work was *Lament for a Nation*—a lament for Canada, which is so vulnerable beside its great imperial neighbor to the south, from which emanates a technological civilization that is in many ways at odds with the beginnings of our Canadian experience in nationhood and our vision, at its best, for a humane and socially conscious alternative to unchecked capitalism. I met George Grant in 1960, through Rhoda, who had become a friend of the whole Grant family at Dalhousie University in Halifax. His *Philosophy in the Mass Age* (Vancouver: Copp Clark, 1959, 1966) and his remarkable collection of essays entitled *Technology and Empire* (Toronto: House of Anansi, 1969) were enormously important for me as I tried to read our zeitgeist, especially in connection with *Lighten Our Darkness*. It is not accidental that George Grant was also, in his basic Christian outlook, attracted to the theology of the cross. See in that connection Harris Athanasiadis, *George Grant and the Theology of the Cross: The Christian Foundations of His Thought* (Toronto: University of Toronto Press, 2001).

28. I owe to Rhoda, as well, my acquaintance with Emil Fackenheim. She and Rose, Emil's once-Protestant wife, had shared rooms in Toronto in the mid-fifties. Emil was himself a refugee from Nazism, having escaped from his German homeland (Halle and Berlin) as a nineteen-year-old candidate for the rabbinate. He taught philosophy at the University of Toronto for many years and moved to Jerusalem only after his retirement from that institution. Of Emil's many books, those that influenced me particularly were *God's Presence in History* (New York: New York University Press, 1970) and *The Religious Dimension in Hegel's Thought* (Boston: Beacon, 1967).

29. In Charles Snow, *The Two Cultures* (New York: Cambridge University Press, 1959).

30. Douglas John Hall, *The Steward: A Biblical Symbol Come of Age* (Grand Rapids: Eerdmans, 1990); *The Stewardship of Life in the Kingdom of Death,* rev. ed. (Grand Rapids: Eerdmans, 1988); and *Imaging God: Dominion as Stewardship* (Grand Rapids: Eerdmans, 1986).

31. Douglas John Hall, *The Reality of the Gospel and the Unreality of the Churches* (Philadelphia: Westminster, 1975).

32. Charles Hodge (1797–1878) was a Presbyterian theologian who taught at Princeton almost the whole of his long life.

33. Dr. Friedrich Hufendiek, now retired and living in Nicholassee/ Berlin, is a minister of the Evangelische Kirche der Union (EKU), successor to the Church of the Prussian Union, created in 1817 by King Frederick William III, who wished to merge Lutheran and Reformed churches in his jurisdiction. In the United States, the Evangelical and Reformed Church, which in 1957 joined with the Congregationalists to form the United Church of Christ in America, was the American continuation of the Church of the Prussian Union. The Niebuhr family stems from this tradition, and one reason why Fritz Hufendiek came to Union Seminary in 1955 as a WCC scholarship student was his attraction to Reinhold Niebuhr's thought. Along with Dietz Lange of the University of Göttingen and Reinhard Neubauer, Fritz has carried Niebuhr's concern for the radical social-ethical consequences of Reformation faith into his work as pastor (chiefly in Bielefeld), university chaplain (Münster/Westphalia), and seminary teacher (Bethel Seminary).

34. Jürgen Moltmann, *Theology of Hope: On the Ground and the Implications of a Christian Eschatology*, trans. James W. Leitch (London: SCM, 1967).

35. The Roman Catholic theologian Gregory Baum, a friend and colleague of many years, notes in a recent autobiographical article for the *Canadian Dimension* that Bloch first came to his attention through a group of German theologians, in particular Johann Baptist Metz of Münster. Bloch, says Baum, distinguished between the "warm current" of Marxism and the "cold, positivistic, or deterministic current." Metz and Moltmann were also in dialogue. It may be said that they represent a Catholic and a Protestant appropriation of Bloch's analysis. Gregory Baum, "My Entry into Critical Political Consciousness," *Canadian Dimension* 38(3) (May/June 2004): 22.

36. In a paper that I wrote for the Canadian Council of Churches, "Towards a Theological Perspective on Human Sexuality," in *Biblical and Theological Understanding of Sexuality and Family Life* (Toronto: Canadian Council of Churches, Faith and Order Commission, November 1969).

37. The essay appeared in *Religion in Life* 40(3) (autumn 1976): 376–90.

38. See Moltmann's essay "Wrestling with God: A Personal Meditation," *Christian Century* (August 13–20, 1997): 726–27.

39. Sydney Mead, *The Lively Experiment: The Shaping of Christianity in America* (New York: Harper and Row, 1963), 145.

40. Ernest Becker, *The Denial of Death* (New York: Free Press, 1973). I consider Becker's book one of the most important works of our epoch. It was written while the author, still a young man, was dying, and it applies to our culture the best insights of the Freudian school of social psychology. I used the work extensively in the first volume of my trilogy, *Thinking the Faith: Christian Theology in a North American Context* (Minneapolis: Fortress Press, 1989), especially 145–96.

41. Buber's final word on the "eclipse of God":

> These last years in a great searching and questioning, seized ever anew by the shudder of the now, I have arrived no further than that I now distinguish a revelation through the hiding of the face, a speaking through the silence. The eclipse of God can be seen with one's eyes, it will be seen. He, however, who today knows nothing other than to say, "See there, it grows lighter!", he leads into error.

Quoted by Fackenheim, *God's Presence in History*, 61.

42. It was Douglas Meeks, then of Eden Seminary, I believe.

43. Jürgen Moltmann, *The Crucified God*, trans. R. A. Wilson and John Bowden (London: SCM, 1974). See also an essay by Moltmann on the same theme, "The Crucified God," *Theology Today* 31 (1974): 6ff., in which he refers to my above-mentioned piece "The Theology of Hope in an Officially Optimistic Society."

44. See Dietrich Bonhoeffer, *The Cost of Discipleship*, trans. R. H. Fuller et al. (London: SCM, 1959), 35ff.

45. "Luther developed his *theologia crucis* as the programme of critical and Reformation theology. *Theologia crucis* is not a single chapter in theology, but the key signature for all Christian theology. It is a completely distinctive kind of theology. It is the point from which all theological statements which seek to be Christian are viewed (W. von Loewenich)." (Moltmann, *The Crucified God*, 72).

46. The reference is to my trilogy, *Thinking the Faith, Professing the Faith, Confessing the Faith*, all having the subtitle *Christian Theology in a North American Context* and published by Fortress Press of Minneapolis in 1989, 1993, and 1996.

47. It is not accidental that the subtitle uses the indefinite and not the definite article: I had and have no illusions about the fact that my work

addresses "a"—not "the"—North American context. *The* North American context is, after all, a great bundle of realities, and no one person is equipped to speak for and to this multiplicity. I have never attempted to represent African Americans, Indigenous, Black, or Asian Canadians, or ethnic and other minorities or marginalized groupings, though I have certainly been conscious of them and have often felt bonds of sympathetic identity with them. Even though I have lived in Quebec since my forty-seventh year, I do not feel competent to speak for francophone Quebec—partly because, living here, I have had to realize precisely how distinctive this society really is. My work assumes my own identity as a member of the historically and culturally dominant component of these two northern nations of our continent, which are Caucasian, largely European in origin, mainly English-speaking in their "New World" forms, deeply modern in orientation, and largely middle-class in terms of their popular expression. While I believe this segment of our continental makeup to be still the dominant segment, it cannot be designated *the* North American context today, for it is surrounded by numerous alternative cultures that differ from it in varying degrees and intensities.

48. Douglas John Hall, *The Cross in Our Context: Jesus and the Suffering World* (Minneapolis: Fortress Press, 2003).

49. "Tradition is the living faith of the dead; traditionalism is the dead faith of the living."

50. The final two parts of this second section differ markedly from the address as it was given originally. Although this results in a certain change of style, especially in the historical generalization, I want to explore the obviously Germanic concentration of this theological tradition in a way that that could not be done in a public forum.

51. I say this despite the fact that there is still among us great admiration for Shakespeare, even for the great bard's tragedies. I suspect that that admiration, so far as it reaches beyond the interests of the chattering classes, has more to do with Shakespeare's extraordinary talent as a poet and shaper of our language and culture than with the actual worldview that he explores and depicts. Nevertheless, as I shall contend in the second part of this section, there has always been an undercurrent in English-speaking culture and art that has known about the "dark side." This countercultural element achieved its most impressive flowering in the late Romantic period (e.g., the novels of Thomas Hardy or the paintings of J. M. W. Turner), but in this as in so many other matters, Shakespeare was a harbinger.

52. "A Mighty Fortress Is Our God"—the Reformation hymn par excellence.

53. One notes, for instance, how important a role is played by "polarities" in the thought of Paul Tillich.

54. It is just this kind of dialectical thinking about Christian faith, I believe, that prompted Reinhold Niebuhr in a little-known 1962 essay on Germany to confess that he thought Lutheran theology "has the most profound religious insights on ultimate questions of human existence." He certainly did not express such a preference out of anything like a Romantic attachment to his own Germanic roots. To the contrary, he was very critical of Lutheranism's abysmal failure to *apply* these theological insights to "problems of political and social morality." Yet Niebuhr obviously felt, as I do, that while the Anglo-Saxon forms of Christianity could be thought superior in their political and social expressions, their theology lacked the depth of exploration and understanding found in Germanic Christianity, particularly that of Luther. See Reinhold Niebuhr, "Germany," *Worldview* (June 1973): 13–18.

55. The Scottish New Testament scholar Matthew Black said to me after a lecture I had given on the theology of the cross that he found this theology "ante-Christian." Not *anti*-Christian, but *ante*-Christian, as though waiting in the anteroom of the church but insufficiently finished doctrinally and in terms of belief to be thought authentically Christian.

56. Martin E. Marty, *Martin Luther* (New York: Viking, 2004), especially 191ff.

57. These are Luther's last written words.

58. The Pauline background of Luther's *theologia crucis* shows through at every point. For instance, in 1 Corinthians 4, Paul chastises the Corinthian Christians for their presumption: they are behaving as if they had already attained the salvation that the apostle himself can only glimpse from afar—a vision for which, indeed, he and his companions must suffer ridicule and worldly rejection:

> Already you have all you want! Already you have become rich! Quite apart from us you have become kings! Indeed, I wish that you had become kings, so that we might be kings with you! For I think that God has exhibited us apostles as last of all, as though sentenced to death, because we have become a spectacle to the world, to angels and to mortals. We are fools for the sake of Christ, but you are wise in Christ. We are weak, but you are strong. You are held in honor,

but we in disrepute. To the present hour we are hungry and thirsty, we are poorly clothed and beaten and homeless, and we grow weary from the work of our own hands. When reviled, we bless; when persecuted, we endure; when slandered, we speak kindly. We have become like the rubbish of the world, the dregs of all things, to this very day. (1 Cor 4:8-13 NRSV)

59. *Time*, March 8, 1948, front cover.

60. Luther, Heidelberg Disputation, Thesis 21.

61. Partly on account of the terrible (and often ludicrous) remarks that Luther sometimes made about Jews, contemporary commentators tend to overlook the fact that his reform was basically a return to the fold of the parental faith of Israel. As Roland Bainton writes in concluding his famous biography of the Reformer, "In his religion he was a Hebrew, not a Greek." Bainton, *Here I Stand: A Life of Martin Luther* (New York and Toronto: New American Library, 1950), 302.

62. William Wordsworth, "Lines Composed a Few Miles above Tintern Abbey."

63. Tillich, *The Courage to Be* (New Haven: Yale Unviversity Press, 1952), 46ff.

64. See, e.g., Jane Jacobs, *Dark Age Ahead* (Toronto: Random House of Canada, 2004).

65. See, e.g., Douglas John Hall, *The End of Christendom and the Future of Christianity* (Eugene, Ore.: Wipf & Stock, 2002); *The Cross in Our Context*, chap. 8; *Thinking the Faith,* chap. 3, sec. 11; *Confessing the Faith*, part II; *The Future of the Church: Has the Church a Future?* (Philadelphia: Westminster Press, 1980); and *The Reality of the Gospel and the Unreality of the Churches.*

66. The word *secularism* was first used by G. J. Holyoake in about 1850 and "denotes a system which seeks to interpret and order life on principles taken solely from this world, without recourse to belief in God and a future life." F. L. Cross, ed., *The Oxford Dictionary of the Christian Church* (Oxford: Oxford University Press, 1983), 1255.

67. See "Statistics," *The Encyclopedia of Protestantism* 4, ed. Hans J. Hillerbrand (New York: Routledge, 2004), 1809ff.

68. Quoting from a digest of the book, "The Next Christianity," *Atlantic Monthly*, October 2002, 57–58.

69. See Russell Botman's essays in *Hope for the World: Mission in a Global Context*, ed. Walter Brueggemann (Louisville: Westminster John Knox, 2001), especially 31ff.

70. Wilfred Cantwell Smith, *The Faith of Other Men* (Toronto: CBC Publications, 1962).

71. Barth, *Evangelical Theology*, 7.

72. This nineteenth-century figure is understood by believers to be the last in a line of divine manifestations; Abraham, Christ, and Muhammad are considered earlier manifestations.

73. See David Lees, "High and Dry," *Canadian Geographic* (May/June 2004): 95ff.

74. Quoted by Basil Willey, *The Seventeenth Century Background* (New York: Doubleday, 1953), 95–96; italics added.

75. Quoted by David Suzuki, "From Naked Ape to Superspecies," CBC Lectures, January 14, 2000. See David Suzuki and Holly Dressel, *From Naked Ape to Superspecies* (Toronto: Stoddart, 1999), 13–14.

76. See Hall, *The Steward.*

77. I developed this thesis most fully in *Imaging God: Dominion as Stewardship,* originally published by Eerdmans in Grand Rapids and now available from Wipf & Stock of Eugene, Oregon (2004). It is also published in French under the title *Être image de Dieu,* trans. Louis Vaillancourt (Paris: Cerf; Montreal: Bellarmin, 1998). I regard it as one of my most important books.

78. Karen Armstrong, *The Battle for God* (New York: Knopf, 2000), 201.

79. See my development of this in *The Cross in Our Context.*

80. See Paul Tillich, *Dynamics of Faith* (New York: Harper & Row, 1957).

81. Miguel de Unamuno, *The Agony of Christianity and Essays on Faith,* trans. Anthony Kerrigan (Princeton, N.J.: Princeton University Press, Bollingen Series 85.5, 1974), 10.

82. Pinchas Lapide, *The Resurrection of Jesus: A Jewish Perspective,* trans. Wilhelm C. Linss (Minneapolis: Augsburg Books, 1983), 127.

83. Joel Blocken, ed., *A Selection of the Best Contemporary Hebrew Writing* (New York: Shocken, 1962), 78.

84. Hans-Joachim Iwand, *Stimme der Gemeinde* 3(4): 1951.

85. See Paul Tillich's *The Protestant Era,* trans. James Luther Adams (Chicago: University of Chicago Press, 1948), 226.

86. Quoted in Marty, *Martin Luther,* 181.

87. Barbara Brown Taylor, *Christian Century* (June 6–13, 2001): 32.

CHAPTER THREE: STEWARDS OF THE MYSTERIES OF GOD

A version of this paper was originally delivered at the Montreat Conference Center in North Carolina in the spring of 2004, as part of the "Reclaiming the Text" series of theological consultations.

1. "Statistics," *The Encyclopedia of Protestantism* 4, ed. Hans J. Hiller-brand (New York: Routledge, 2004), 1809–16.

2. *The Encyclopedia of Protestantism* 1, 347.

3. As noted earlier, the historian of doctrine, Jaroslav Pelikan, has wisely contrasted "traditionalism" and "tradition" in this way: tradition is the living faith of the dead; traditionalism is the dead faith of the living.

4. Paul Tillich, *Systematic Theology*, vol. 2 (Chicago: University of Chicago Press, 1957), 97.

5. See my discussion of H. Richard Niebuhr in Douglas John Hall, *Remembered Voices: Reclaiming the Legacy of "Neo-Orthodoxy"* (Louisville: Westminster John Knox, 1998), especially 98.

6. "Evangelical theology is an eminently *critical* science, for it is continually exposed to judgment and never relieved of the crisis in which it is placed by its object, or, rather to say, by its living subject." Karl Barth, *Evangelical Theology: An Introduction*, trans. Grover Foley (New York: Holt, Rinehart and Winston, 1963), 10.

7. *Anselm's Fides Quaerens Intellectum* (London: SCM, 1960), 24.

8. Blaise Pascal, *Pensées,* no. 273.

9. This is an issue I address in this book's introduction.

10. Ronald Goetz, "Protestant Houses of God: A Contradiction in Terms?" *Christian Century* (March 20–27, 1985): 299.

11. E. Theodore Bachman, introduction, in *Word and Sacrament*, pt. 1, *Luther's Works* (Philadelphia: Muhlenberg, 1960), vol. 35, part I, 116.

12. See my essay "The Diversity of Christian Witnessing in the Tension between Word and Relation to the Context," in *Luther's Ecumenical Significance*, ed. Carter Lindberg and Harry McSorley (Philadelphia: Fortress Press, 1984). The original German title of the essay, one assigned me, was *"Die Vielgestaltigkeit christlichen Zeugnisses im Spannungsfeld zwischen Wortgebundeheit und Contextbezug."* I think the German title captures more accurately the dialectic under discussion. It can be found in the German edition of the work, entitled *Oekumenische Erschliessung Martin Luthers*, ed. Peter Manns and Harding Meyer (Paderborn: Verlag Bonifatius un. Verla Otto Lembeck, 1982).

13. Miguel de Unamuno, *The Agony of Christianity and Essays on*

Faith, trans. Anthony Kerrigan (Princeton, N.J.: Princeton University Press, Bollingen Series 85.5, 1974), 10.

14. Paul Tillich, *Dynamics of Faith* (New York: Harper & Row, 1957), 21.

15. Gustav Aulen, *Christus Victor: An Historical Study of the Three Main Types of the Idea of Atonement*, trans. A. G. Hebert (London: SPCK, 1953).

CHAPTER FOUR: WORDS

This chapter was originally a sermon preached in 2002 at Trinity Lutheran Seminary in Columbus, Ohio.

1. German publication by Hermann Luchterhand Verlag of Darmstadt and Neuwied, 1979. First published in England in 1981 by Martin Secker & Warburg of London, 1981, translated by Ralph Mannheim.

CHAPTER FIVE: DE PROFUNDIS

This chapter is excerpted from my acceptance address for the 2003 Book of the Year award at the meeting of the Academy of Parish Clergy, Cleveland, Ohio, April 28, 2004.

1. Biographical detail at the beginning of Wodehouse's *Psmith in the City* (Harmondsworth: Penguin, 1910).

2. *The Living Thoughts of Kierkegaard*, presented by W. H. (Bloomington: Indiana Unviersity Press, 1966), 30.

3. "Buecher, die uns gluecklich machen, konnten wir zur Not selber schreiben." This quote is from a letter to Oskar Pollak, January 27, 1904:

Altogether, I think we ought to read only books that bite and sting us. If the book does not shake us awake like a blow to the skull, why bother reading it in the first place? So that it can make us happy, as you put it? Good God, we'd be just as happy if we had no books at all; books that make us happy we could, in a pinch, also write ourselves. What we need are books that hit us like a most painful misfortune, like the death of someone we loved more than ourselves, that make us feel as though we had been banished to the woods, far from any human presence, like a suicide. A book must be the ax for the frozen sea within us. That is what I believe. (www.themodernword.com/kafka/kafka_quotes.html)

4. Douglas John Hall, *The Cross in Our Context: Jesus and the Suffering World* (Minneapolis: Fortress Press, 2003).

Index

Dietrich, Suzanne de, 34, 42
divinity, 34
Dostoyevsky, Fyodor, 128
doubt, 116–18
dualism, 67–68

Encyclopedia of Protestantism, 15,
  106–7
Endo, Shusaku, 61
environmental issues, 95–96
evangelism, 76
exclusivism, 88–89
existentialism, 64

faith, 35, 99–105, 110–11, 113–18
Falke, Heino, 48
Frankenheim, Emil, 143 n.28
fundamentalism, 76

Gibson, Mel, 119
Goetz, Ronald, 114
Golwitzer, Helmut, 53, 54
grace, 110–11
Grant, Frederick, 36
Grant, George P., 143 n.27
Grass, Günter, 38, 122–25
Great Depression (1930s), 76–77

Hall, Douglas John
  autobiography by, 27–31
  Confessing the Faith, 62
  The Cross in Our Context, 62,
    79
  fatherhood, 46
  The Future of the Church, 48,
    136 n.4
  Imaging God, 149 n.77
  influences, 32–38, 47, 75–81
  Lighten Our Darkness, 45, 60

in 1960s, 38–42
  Professing the Faith, 62
  The Reality of the Gospel and
    the Unreality of the
    Churches, 48
  Remembered Voices, 34–35
  and science, 47–48
  students, 49–50
  as theologian, future, 82–105
  as theologian, past, 11–12,
    32–50
  as theologian, present, 51–81
  Thinking the Faith, 62
  vocation of, 7–12, 27–105
  Why Christian? 136 n.4
Hall, Keith, 136 n.4
Hamel, Joseph, 48
Handy, Robert, 36
Heidegger, Martin, 64
Hesse, Hermann, 42
Hobbes, Thomas, 96
Hodge, Charles, 52
Hoekendijk, J. C., 39
Hook, Sydney, 56
hope, theology of, 52–58
hospitality, 90–91
Hufendiek, Friedrich, 52–53,
    56, 59
humanity, 34

imperialism, 43–44
inclusivism, 89
irrationalism, 113–15
Iwand, Hans-Joachim, 53, 54,
    103

Jeffries, Arthur, 36
Jenkins, Philip, 84
Jesus Christ, 91–92

See also theology, Christian

rationalism, 113–15
realism, 72
Reformation, 16
Richardson, Cyril, 36
Ricoeur, Paul, 29
Roberts, David, 36
Robinson, J. A. T., 39–40
Roosevelt, Franklin, 57
Rupp, Gordon, 141 n.22

Sartre, Jean-Paul, 64
Sayers, Dorothy, 42
Scherer, Paul, 35
science, 47–48
Scriptures
    about, 115–16
    1 Corinthians 4:1, 108
    1 Corinthians 9:16, 4
    1 Corinthians 12:4-5, 1
    1 Corinthians 12:27-13:1, 1
    Ecclesiastes 1:2-3, 80
    Genesis 11, 101
    Hebrews 11:1, 117
    Jeremiah 20:7-9, 5–6
    Job 38:2, 15
    John 14:6, 6
    John 21:18, 6
    1 Peter 3:15, 108
    Psalms 24:1, 98
    Romans 3:21, 51
    Romans 4:17, 133
    Romans 7:21, 68
secularism, 83–84
September 11, 2001 terrorist
    attacks, 43, 71, 87, 100
Shakespeare, William, 128
Sifton, Elizabeth, 141 n.21

simplism, 111–13
sin, 119
Smith, Wilfred Cantwell, 87–88
Snow, Charles, 48
Socrates, 28
Soelle, Dorothee, 10, 61, 75
Song, C. S., 61
Spong, John, 40
Stackhouse, John G., 107
stewardship, 94–99, 106–21

Taylor, Barbara Brown, 104
teaching ministry, 7–9, 13, 114
Terrien, Samuel, 36
theologia crucis. See cross,
    theology of
theology, Christian, 18–26
    beyond, 83–86
    changes in, 31
    dialectical character, 111–13
    disintegration of, 8, 13
    Germanic background,
        64–67, 73
    and justification, 73
    neo-orthodox, 34–38
    origin of word, 14
    preserving, 14, 106–21
    as theology of the cross, 50,
        59–75
    types of, 41
    as vocation, 1–17
t'Hooft, W. A. Visser, 142 n.24
Thoreau, Henry David, 78
Tillich, Paul, 8, 34, 36, 37, 42, 45,
    75, 103, 109, 117, 118
time, 51–52
Toffler, Alvin, 55
Tolstoy, Leo, 128
Tower of Babel, 101